KRIEGSMARINE ATLANTIC COMMAND 1939–42

Naval Group West's surface menace

Lawrence Paterson

Illustrated by Jim Laurier

OSPREY PUBLISHING
Bloomsbury Publishing Plc
Kemp House, Chawley Park, Cumnor Hill, Oxford OX2 9PH, UK
Bloomsbury Publishing Ireland Limited,
29 Earlsfort Terrace, Dublin 2, D02 AY28, Ireland
1385 Broadway, 5th Floor, New York, NY 10018, USA
E-mail: info@ospreypublishing.com
www.ospreypublishing.com

OSPREY is a trademark of Osprey Publishing Ltd

First published in Great Britain in 2025

A catalogue record for this book is available from the British Library.

ISBN: PB 9781472867377; eBook 9781472867391; ePDF 9781472867360; XML 9781472867384

25 26 27 28 29   10 9 8 7 6 5 4 3 2 1

Maps by www.bounford.com
Diagrams by Adam Tooby
Index by Angela Hall
Typeset by PDQ Digital Media Solutions, Bungay, UK
Printed by Repro India Ltd

Front Cover: Art by Jim Laurier, © Osprey Publishing

Osprey Publishing supports the Woodland Trust, the UK's leading woodland conservation charity.

To find out more about our authors and books visit www.ospreypublishing.com. Here you will find
extracts, author interviews, details of forthcoming events and the option to sign up for our newsletter.

For product safety related questions contact productsafety@bloomsbury.com

CONTENTS

THE FLEET'S PURPOSE

At 0448hrs on 1 September 1939, the elderly battleship *Schleswig Holstein*, whose lineage stretched back to the turn of the century Imperial German Navy and which was now a training vessel, followed orders from Berlin and opened fire on Polish fortifications on the Westerplatte Peninsular, near Danzig. With these shots, *Schleswig Holstein* initiated a war for which the Kriegsmarine was woefully unprepared and which commanding officer Erich Raeder had been repeatedly assured by his commander-in-chief would not begin until 1944 at the earliest.

The Great War had ended in 1918 with much of the Imperial German Navy in revolutionary chaos, a state into which it periodically lapsed during the turbulent decade that followed. The accension of *Admiral* Erich Raeder to the head of the Reichsmarine (*Chefs der Marineleitung*) in October 1928 can fairly be seen as a positive turning point in the arduous reconstruction of the navy both materially and mentally. The morale of the navy had been dealt heavy blows not only by its unfortunate dalliance with political turmoil and scandal, but also by the severe limitations placed upon it by the terms of the Versailles Treaty. Limited to 15,000 men, the Reichsmarine was to possess no U-boats and the surface fleet was limited to six pre-dreadnought battleships (plus two in reserve), six light cruisers (plus another two in reserve), 12 destroyers, and 12 torpedo boats (each type with an extra four in reserve). Any replacements for the outdated battleships were restricted to a maximum of 10,000-tons displacement. This latter restriction would initiate the design of a new class of capital ship, known as *Panzerschiffe*. The term capital ship generally does not include cruisers, and though these vessels were later reclassified as heavy cruisers, their unique combination of features led to them most famously being known by the British press as 'pocket battleships'.

Originally, two alternative designs were considered for the allowable replacements for Germany's outdated battleships. The first was a slow, well-armoured monitor-type coastal defence vessel or fast medium-armed and armoured ship that would be more versatile. After spirited discussions within Naval Command, the latter was chosen: a cruiser type with a main battery of six 28cm guns in two triple turrets, and a speed of 26 knots. This new *Panzerschiff* would be slower than equivalent tonnage heavy cruisers of foreign navies but its firepower, armoured protection and range would be superior, the latter due to the decision to use diesel rather than steam propulsion. Construction of '*Panzerschiff A*' (originally slated to be named *Preussen*, but later named *Deutschland*) began on 5 February 1929, followed by '*Panzerschiff B*' (*Admiral Scheer*) and '*Panzerschiff C*' (*Admiral Graf Spee*) in 1931 and 1932 respectively.

Adolf Hitler at the launching of new battleship *Scharnhorst* in 1936. Immediately behind Hitler is *Generalfeldmarschall* Werner von Blomberg, head of the German Armed Forces (*Wehrmacht*). To the left is *Grossadmiral* Erich Raeder who had been appointed Commander-in-Chief (C-in-C) of the Navy in 1928 and would serve in this post until his resignation in January 1943. (Hulton Archive/Getty Images)

Raeder placed great emphasis on sweeping away sour memories of the previous years by ensuring that the navy gave unquestioning support to Germany's government, no matter its composition, provided that the ruling party represented the will of the German people. Upon Hitler's appointment to the position of Chancellor in January 1933, the three services of the Wehrmacht were now answerable to a leader determined to restore their power and prestige. A short time after his appointment, Hitler met with Raeder to discuss the preparedness of the navy. He informed the Admiral that he desired peace with England, Italy and Japan at all costs, and that the role of the German Navy lay 'within the framework of its responsibilities toward European continental policy'.[1] He also claimed no desire to challenge Britain's dominance at sea, but rather planned to reach an Anglo-German agreement to fix relative naval strengths. Therefore, as Raeder noted, with the Russian Navy insignificant, by a simple process of elimination France was left as a potential future enemy.

The following year a referendum was presented to the German people that resulted in the merging of the post of Chancellor and President; the new title of *Führer und Reichskanzler* (Führer and Chancellor) finally gave Hitler total dictatorial power over Germany. Rearmament subsequently intensified. During 1933 Germany had withdrawn from the League of Nations, and in 1935 Hitler formally repudiated the Treaty of Versailles and announced overt German rearmament following years of covert development both within Germany and beyond its borders. Fearing that French intransigence would once again provoke a German-led European arms race of the kind that resulted in war in 1914,

---

1 Raeder, p. 166.

In 1935 Adolf Hitler formally announced German rearmament, ending the restrictions of the Versailles Treaty. The Kriegsmarine was among his resurgent military, with ambitious recruitment and construction schemes. Here Kriegsmarine sailors take part in the 'Grand Tattoo' that marked the last 'Wehrmacht Day' of the 1935 Nuremberg Party Congress – the so-called 'Rally of Freedom'. (AC)

Britain signed the bilateral deal that Hitler had desired on 18 June 1935, that became the Anglo-German Naval Agreement. In tacit acknowledgement of Germany's flagrant breach of the Versailles Treaty, the agreement limited the Kriegsmarine's size to 35 per cent of that of the Royal Navy, though there was a specific clause that gave Germany 'the right to possess a submarine tonnage equal to the total submarine tonnage possessed by the Members of the British Commonwealth of Nations'.

This agreement, which provoked strong French condemnation, was designed to allay fears within Britain of German expansionist aims in Europe. Following assurances from Hitler that war with Britain was unlikely, Raeder pushed ahead with plans for construction of a balanced fleet that favoured surface vessels over U-boats. In this drive, Raeder showed an unwillingness to adapt new theoretical doctrine for the resurging navy, but rather continued along a reactionary path to establish a blue water navy. Perhaps part of this drive had stemmed from comments made by Hitler in the *Völkischer Beobachter* on 21 October 1932 where he criticized costly and time-consuming naval construction of major ships that could 'confuse the foreign policy view' by causing concern in France and Britain. Fearing the relegation of German naval power to a mere coastguard, and in direct contravention of some previously held views in which he questioned construction of anything beyond defensive craft for the Baltic and North Seas, Raeder thereafter remained somewhat fixated on the supreme power of capital ships.

Despite a parallel drive to establish a naval air arm, he may never have fully appreciated the shift in the balance of power away from major surface units towards naval aviation; and at any rate was thwarted by *Reichsmarschall* Herman Göring's vanity and cast-iron grip on Germany's air forces.

On 24 May 1938 Hitler signalled a major change in foreign and military policy following British and French reaction to the Czechoslovakian crisis. Raeder was informed by Hitler's naval adjutant *Kapitänleutnant* Karl Jesko von Puttkamer that, though he considered them unlikely to go to war over Czechoslovakia, the Führer now considered Britain and France to be Germany's 'bitterest enemies' and ordered a crash programme of naval production concentrating on U-boats and surface ships suitable for cruiser warfare against Britain.[2] That June, Raeder directed his staff to explore the implications of war with Britain. Among the conclusions reached was the necessity of concentrating on high-seas commerce warfare, most suited to *Panzerschiffe*, cruisers and U-boats. The application of battleships to this type of warfare was studied, but with contradictory results. While all naval

---

2 'The May Crisis of 1938: A Rejoinder to Mr Wallace', D. C. Watt, T*he Slavonic and East European Review*, Vol. 44, No. 103 (Jul. 1966), pp. 475–480.

The new *Panzerschiff* (known to the British as pocket battleships) *Admiral Graf Spee* passes under the Levensau High Bridge that spans the Kiel Canal. *Graf Spee* was commissioned into the German Fleet in January 1936, becoming the flagship of the Kriegsmarine. (AC)

staff agreed on the necessity of possessing battleships, they could not reach agreement on how best to employ them.

The final draft of the so-called 'Z-Plan' of Raeder's emergency construction schedule was not presented to Hitler until 17 January 1939, intended for completion by 1948. Though conflict with France – considered a second-tier naval power – had been thought possible, by Hitler's earliest reckoning, potential war with Britain was unlikely to begin before 1944 and consensus was reached between Hitler, Raeder and SKL (*Seekriegsleitung*), that the Kriegsmarine would be ready for Atlantic warfare by June 1936 with six super-heavy H-class battleships, four carriers, four heavy cruisers and 247 U-boats, as well as large numbers of smaller warships and auxiliary craft.

Raeder envisioned the completed programme allowing two fleet battlegroups, each consisting of three battleships and supporting ships, engaging and destroying Royal Navy heavy units which would themselves be engaged in hunting German merchant raiders, while other battleships remained in home waters to tie down covering Royal Navy forces. However, by January 1939 the Z-Plan completion date was brought forward to 1944, and in April Hitler repudiated the Anglo-German Naval Agreement of 1935 that had sought to curb a naval arms race during a bellicose speech given in the Reichstag, and war edged ever nearer.

German naval development was hampered more by their shipbuilding capacity than by international limitations. Göring's assertion that British and French naval power could be comprehensively checked by his Luftwaffe did little to assist Raeder's drive for construction priorities. Eventually, as war became increasingly likely, Raeder revised his Z-Plan with a priority list of construction to create a fleet capable of damaging Britain's merchant tradelines rather than traditional major fleet actions. Raeder envisioned single battleships and cruisers operating as merchant raiders, as well as U-boats, though he had failed to grasp the full potential of the U-boat service until the last moment.

Despite a commerce war now being the fleet's *raison d'être*, early relationships between the High Seas Fleet and U-boat service remained strained, resulting in initially little cooperation between the two. Naval doctrine that had focused on surface engagements with enemy warships – something that would be reflected in the armour configuration aboard German battleships – was rapidly revised. Ironically, the most powerful German units such as *Bismarck* were less than ideal for their new role, reflecting the design choices stemming from confusion over the ships' clear purpose.

On 1 September 1939 the German Fleet consisted of:

2 commissioned battleships (*Scharnhorst* and *Gneisenau*)
2 battleships nearing constructive completion (*Bismarck* and *Tirpitz*)
3 *Panzerschiffe* (pocket battleships) (*Admiral Graf Spee*, *Admiral Scheer* and *Deutschland*)
3 heavy cruisers (*Admiral Hipper*, *Blücher* and *Prinz Eugen*)
5 light cruisers (*Königsberg*, *Nürnberg*, *Leipzig*, *Köln* and *Karlsruhe*)
20 destroyers (grouped in four flotillas)
12 torpedo boats (grouped in two flotillas)
17 S-boats (grouped in two flotillas)
57 U-boats (grouped in six flotillas)
Minesweepers (including militarily purpose-built ships, R-boats, auxiliary converted trawlers)
Sperrbrecher mine clearance vessels
Patrol boats (generally converted trawlers) and the various smaller security vessels
Additionally, 26 merchant ships were to be converted to auxiliary cruisers at the outbreak of hostilities; not beforehand in order to avoid any possibility of raising international suspicion regarding Germany's military ambitions.

With such a slender force available, major surface elements of the Kriegsmarine were now instructed to avoid fleet actions and concentrate on their roles as surface merchant raiders. To that end, the *Panzerschiffe Admiral Graf Spee* and *Deutschland* both departed Germany during August, on the 21st and 24th respectively. They had been preceded by a supply ship each – *Altmark* and *Westerwald* – in preparation for lengthy voyages. *Altmark* had been the first to leave, *Korvettenkapitän der Reserve* Heinrich Dau taking his ship from Germany on 5 August, travelling through the English Channel with provisions and spare parts though bound for a refinery in Port Arthur in Texas, USA, to take on diesel oil. While *Graf Spee* traversed north of Britain through the Faroe Islands Gap and headed for a waiting position in the South Atlantic west of the Cape Verde Islands, *Deutschland* was passed through the Denmark Strait and stationed in the North Atlantic south-east of Greenland's southern tip. Both had received orders that, in the event of war, they were to carry out the 'disruption and destruction of enemy merchant shipping by all possible means'.[3] Furthermore, 'enemy naval forces, even if inferior, are only to be engaged if it should

---

3   Operational Orders for *Deutschland* and *Admiral Graf Spee*, issued by SKL, 4 August 1939.

further the principal task (i.e. war on merchant shipping). Frequent changes in the operational area will provoke uncertainty and delays in the sailing of enemy shipping, even if no material success is achieved. The temporary appearance of German warships in remote areas will add to the enemy's confusion.' On 31 August, Hitler issued 'Directive Number 1 for the Conduct of War'. In it, he wrote: 'The Navy will carry on warfare against merchant shipping, directed mainly at England.'

(Right to left) Hitler, Raeder, *Generaloberst* Wilhelm Keitel (head of OKW, Armed Forces High Command) and *Reichsminister* Dr Hans Heinrich Lammers (Chief of the Reich Chancellery) aboard the *Panzerschiff Deutschland* in 1939. (DPA Picture Alliance/Alamy Stock Photo)

On 3 September 1939, as Britain and France declared war on Germany, Raeder reflected on the situation his Kriegsmarine now faced, writing his thoughts for posterity in a document co-signed by Kurt Assmann, head of the German Naval Archive. Within these paragraphs he stated that the *Panzerschiffe*, though not capable of deciding the war's outcome, could at least hope to carry out high seas cruiser warfare at 'least for some time'. Overall, though, he baldly stated that his surface forces were so weak in the face of Royal Navy opposition that 'even at full strength, they can do no more than show that they know how to die gallantly and thus are willing to create the foundations for later reconstruction.' Events would prove him substantially correct. Ironically, perhaps, his rumination also shows a lack of clear understanding of the politics of the day. He had detailed knowledge of the impending attack on Poland – which was, after all, opened by an obsolete Kriegsmarine vessel – but chose to believe vague assurances from the Führer over clear evidence of German territorial ambition.

With what he already had available to him, Raeder knew that major fleet actions were to be avoided as the Kriegsmarine waged a war on merchant shipping. Correspondingly, U-boat production was belatedly increased, though would not meet Karl Dönitz's, *Führer der Unterseeboote* (FdU), requirements until too late in the course of the war. While future battleship construction was postponed, those either in service or nearing completion were to be tasked with long-range commerce raiding missions. Lightly defended convoys would be fruitful targets for heavy German ships and by attacking these Raeder hoped to force the Royal Navy to strengthen convoy escort requirements, possibly leading to fewer convoys sailing, to the corresponding detriment of supply imports to Britain. Combat with enemy naval forces was only to be undertaken 'if it should further the principal task (i.e. war on merchant shipping)'.[4] Though the first two heavy surface ships had already headed to their waiting positions, both *Deutschland* and *Admiral Graf Spee* were ordered not to begin operations on Hitler's express instructions until the 'political situation' with Britain and France was clearer as they appeared to be acting cautiously as Poland neared capitulation. It was an inauspicious beginning.

---

4   Führer Conferences, p. 35.

FLEET FIGHTING POWER

THE HIGH SEAS FLEET (*FLOTTENSTREITKRÄFTE*)

Battleships: *Scharnhorst*; *Gneisenau*; *Bismarck* and *Tirpitz*

Scharnhorst's forward control tower, with a 10.5m rangefinder at its top, seen from abreast the funnel looking forward. (Naval Heritage and History Command)

Following the 1935 Anglo-German Naval Agreement, Germany was permitted to build a surface fleet of up to 35 per cent of that of Britain, allowing battleship tonnage of 183,000 tons to be constructed. Naval command subsequently announced, on 9 July 1935, the laying down of keels for two battleships: *Scharnhorst* and *Gneisenau* in Wilhelmshaven and Kiel respectively. They were designed to counter the latest French fast battleships *Dunkerque* and *Strasbourg* (often referred to as battlecruisers) that outclassed the three *Panzerschiffe* already under construction.

Scharnhorst and *Gneisenau* would be as well-armoured as the French ships, but slightly faster after the choice was made to power them using steam turbines. While the diesel engines that had been developed for *Panzerschiffe* proved extremely successful and provided a wide cruising range, high-temperature, high-pressure steam turbines were chosen for the two battleships, though without the benefit of extensive trials. Raeder was loathe to delay construction of the two ships to properly test the newly designed installations and, aware of the advances already made in the similar powerplant installed aboard the cruiser *Prinz Eugen* over older versions aboard the preceding cruisers *Blücher* and *Admiral Hipper*, opted for the turbines over diesel engines. Aware that they could never hope to match the fuel economy of the diesel powerplants aboard the *Panzerschiffe*, Raeder considered the smaller space requirement and higher speeds of these new high-pressure, high-temperature steam installations to be a major step in the development of such a machine which would satisfy all Kriegsmarine requirements.

Scharnhorst was therefore powered by three Brown, Boveri & Cie geared steam turbines, which gave a maximum speed of 31.5 knots on speed trials, slightly surpassing *Gneisenau* which carried three Germania geared steam turbines and reached a maximum speed of 31.3 knots on similar trials.

Both ships possessed an armour belt 350mm (13.8in) thick flanking the central area where it protected ammunition magazines and propulsion machinery spaces. An armoured deck 20–40mm thick covered the flat deck area, increasing to 105mm as it sloped down to meet the armoured belt. The three main gun turrets were protected by 360mm armoured facia, the sides 200mm thick. The conning tower was protected by 350mm of armour on each side.

However, the punch provided to the 1934 battleship designs was limited due to political considerations. While tonnage was increased to allow greater armoured protection, the militarily desirable aspect of upgrading to 38cm SK C/34 main armament was not deemed politically acceptable by Hitler in the international climate at that time, lest it be viewed as a violation of disarmament conditions, and the Führer refused Raeder's request to provide larger calibre main guns to his ships. Ultimately, such an upgrade would not have been particularly practical anyway, requiring as it would have, a full redesign of the hull with corresponding constructive delay.

Both ships were armed with nine 28cm SK C/34 guns arranged in three triple gun turrets. Two turrets – 'Anton' and 'Bruno' – were mounted forward and one – Caesar – aft. An improved weapon over that fitted to the *Panzerschiffe*, the high muzzle velocity gave its relatively lightweight shells long range and good penetration power against belt armour. In fact, *Scharnhorst* made one of the longest hits ever scored by a naval gun during the sinking of HMS *Glorious* in 1940 at a range of approximately 24,200m.

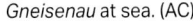
Gneisenau at sea. (AC)

Secondary armament consisted of 12 15cm SK C/28 guns, eight of which were placed in two-gun turrets and the remaining four mounted in individual turrets. Though an effective weapon, the decision to not utilize multi-purpose guns that could tackle both anti-ship and anti-aircraft roles was considered wasteful of

space and weight. Instead, anti-aircraft armament consisted of 14 10.5cm SK C/33 guns (possible to use against surface targets if required), 16 3.7cm SK C/30 semi-automatic (and thus slow rate of fire) guns and, initially, 10 2cm C/30 anti-aircraft guns, which possessed a small magazine of only 20 rounds and were thus paused for frequent reloading. The number of 2cm guns was eventually increased to 38. Later, in 1942, six 53.3cm (21in) above-water torpedo tubes, taken from the light cruisers *Nürnberg* and *Leipzig*, were installed.

Gneisenau was commissioned first on 21 May 1938, *Scharnhorst* on 7 January 1939. During sea trials both ships revealed a dangerous tendency to ship considerable amounts of water in heavy seas due to their straight perpendicular stem. This caused flooding in the bow section and damaged electrical systems within the forward gun turret. Subsequent dockyard modification fitted a raised Atlantic bow. A raked funnel cap was also fitted as well as some other relatively minor superstructure modifications before both ships were declared fully operational.

Of Germany's modest number of battleships during World War II, one name undoubtedly is remembered above all others: *Bismarck*. One of the heavy 'sisters', the other being *Tirpitz*, *Bismarck* was to that point the heaviest ship launched by the Kriegsmarine, displacing 50,300 metric tons under full load. However, its popular fame has somewhat eclipsed the reality of its service.

Bismarck was indeed a fine ship, which prompted Winston Churchill to say in November 1939 that its arrival into the Atlantic war would be 'disastrous in the highest degree, as it can neither be caught nor killed, and would therefore range freely throughout the oceans, rupturing all communications'.[5] However, it was a ship that was relatively unsuited for its eventual employment. Designed to combat the Royal Navy in traditional battleship-vs-battleship action, it possessed insufficient range to act as an Atlantic raider. Though capable of an impressive 30.01 knots in trials, its range was 8,870nm at 19 knots. The former compares favourably to the likes of the *Admiral Graf Spee's* top speed of 28.5 knots, but the issue or endurance pales next to *Graf Spee's* 16,300nm range at 18.7 knots. More than any other Kriegsmarine ship, *Bismarck* would be wholly dependent on access to supply ships. During its testing period – curtailed by severe winter weather interfering with an already rushed timetable – the *Artillerieversuchskommando für Schiffe* (Naval Ordnance Testing Command for Warships, or AVKS) compiled a 106-page report listing deficiencies in both the battleship's main weaponry and, perhaps more crucially, its flak weaponry and control systems, the *Bismarck* being equipped with the upgraded SL-8 anti-aircraft fire control system that had not yet been fully developed and tested.

Nevertheless, *Bismarck* packed a powerful punch with eight of the 38cm SK C/34s that had been vetoed for *Scharnhorst* and *Gneisenau*. These were housed in four heavily armoured twin turrets alphabetically arranged from bow to stern:

---

5   Churchill War Cabinet Paper 116, 3 November 1939, quoted in *The Churchill War Papers, Volume 1: At the Admiralty, September 1939–May 1940*, Martin Gilbert, ed. (New York: W. W. Norton, 1993), p. 328.

'Anton', 'Bruno', 'Caesar' and 'Dora'. The secondary (anti-destroyer) armament comprised 12 15cm SK C/28 guns in three twin turrets either side of the ship. For its flak defence *Bismarck* carried 16 10.5cm SK C/33 guns in four double mounts on each side, 16 3.7cm SK C/30 guns in four double mounts on each side, 10 2cm MG C/30 guns in single pedestal mounts, two in single mounts and eight 2cm Flak C/38s in two quadruple mounts (*Vierling*) that were installed in April 1941.

Bismarck was powered by three Blohm & Voss steam turbines, each serving a single propeller shaft tipped by propellors 4.7m in diameter. Two parallel rudders provided steerage, though it was noted in exercises that while simulating rudder failure, the ship was extremely difficult to steer by using the engines alone; something at which comparable Allied ships fared better as they generally carried four propellor shafts.

The sister ship to the vaunted *Bismarck* – *Tirpitz* – never entered the Atlantic Ocean and, in fact only ever fired its main guns in anger at a surface target during a shore bombardment of Spitzbergen in September 1943. Instead, the ship was used as a perpetual threat to Arctic convoys until the day it was finally capsized by Allied bombing on 12 November 1944.

Panzerschiffe: Deutschland (later renamed Lützow); Admiral Scheer and Admiral Graf Spee

The 'pocket battleship' concept was a direct result of German naval design under Versailles Treaty limitations as well as the effects of the Washington Naval Treaty signed on 6 February 1922 that limited armaments at sea. Battleships' main guns were restricted to 16in/40cm while cruisers should not exceed 10,000 tons and have main guns over 8in/20cm. While the maximum battleship tonnage allowed under Versailles' terms was 10,000 tons – generally the size of an ordinary light cruiser – German designers rose to the challenge of squeezing every possible feature into a compact design which fell between a cruiser and battleship; perfectly balancing speed, defensive capability and firepower.

Gneisenau moored for gunnery practice to the two concrete pontoons constructed by the Kriegsmarine south-west of Brest harbour near the mouth of the Aulne River. Known at the time as the *Ducs de l'Aulne* they are now called the 'Bismarck Blocks' as they had been constructed so that Brest could accommodate the *Bismarck* rather than having to use St Nazaire. (AC)

Deutschland photographed during the Spanish Civil War as part of the international non-interventionist patrol. The red, white and black stripes on the turrets are peculiar to this role. *Deutschland* was bombed by Republican aircraft on 24 May 1937, killing 31 sailors. In retaliation, *Admiral Scheer* shelled Almería. (AC)

Though the three *Panzerschiffe* differed slightly in size – and would all eventually overrun the 10,000-ton limitation – they shared the same design characteristics. The hull was constructed of a transverse steel frame and was 90 per cent welded rather than being traditionally riveted, which saved 15 per cent of the total hull weight. Propulsion by two sets of four 9-cylinder, double-acting, two-stroke MAN diesel engines also saved weight, as well as providing a top speed of over 28 knots and an extended operating range due to their superb fuel economy. These 54,000bhp diesel engines turned twin screws and provided the ships with full power at a moment's notice, as opposed to the more orthodox steam-turbine ships that required time to raise steam from cruising to maximum speed.

However, the same handicap that limited firepower aboard *Scharnhorst* and *Gneisenau* was applied to the *Panzerschiffe*. Their main armament comprised six 28cm (11in) SK C/28 guns mounted in two armoured triple-turrets, one at either end of the main superstructure. These could fire a 300kg projectile at a muzzle velocity of 910m/s, outgunning the standard 8in (20.3cm) guns found on most heavy cruisers of the era. As the third of the trio was approved for construction in December 1933, Hitler remained steadfastly unwilling to risk upsetting his hoped-for Anglo–German Naval Agreement by increasing the firepower of the *Panzerschiffe*. Unwilling to openly violate Versailles Treaty conditions, he went only as far as to allow design plans to be drawn up for a third triple gun turret to be added, which never reached fruition.

A secondary armament of eight 15cm SK C/28 guns in single midships turrets and eight 53.3cm (21in) torpedo tubes placed in two quadruple launchers mounted on the stern gave the ships a punch well above the expected. Anti-aircraft weapons were in an almost constant state of upgrade and by 1940 had reached six 10.5cm L/65 guns, four 3.7cm SK C/30 guns and, initially, 10 2cm flak guns.

The presence of *Admiral Graf Spee* in tropical waters during 1939 presented fresh challenges for ammunition storage. Cooled by carbon dioxide, it was the domain of specialist engineers to keep the ammunition bunkers at a steady temperature lest they overheat. Hans Langsdorff, captain of the *Admiral Graf Spee*, was particularly convinced that such overheating had been the cause of a spontaneous ammunition explosion aboard Word War I's SMS *Karlsruhe*, which was sunk by the blast on 4 November 1914 near Barbados.

The ships' main armoured belt was 80mm thick amidships and thinned to 60mm on either end of the central citadel; underwater protection consisted of a 45mm thick torpedo bulkhead, reduced to 40mm on *Admiral Scheer* and *Admiral Graf Spee*. Armoured decks ranged between 17 to 45mm.

Though not designed to carry aircraft – forbidden under Versailles – they were all later converted to do so; *Deutschland* becoming in 1935 the first German warship to install a catapult and cranes capable of handling a Heinkel He 60 floatplane (later changed to an Arado Ar195). Such aircraft were useful both for reconnaissance and artillery spotting for fall of shot during an engagement.

The construction of these ships was faced with some major political opposition during the turbulent final years of the Weimar government, particularly by Social Democrats, who campaigned for election with the slogan 'Food not *Panzerkreuzer*'. International pressure also mounted once the design details had become known and Allied nations unsuccessfully attempted to have their construction halted. However, as they technically fell within the prescribed Versailles Treaty limitations, the three ships were completed, the last, *Admiral Graf Spee*, launched on 30 June 1934 and was formally commissioned into the Kriegsmarine on 6 January 1936. Plans for an additional two *Panzerschiffe* – named *Ersatz Elsass* and *Ersatz Hessen* after the two obsolete ships they were to replace – were shelved in 1935. Designated D-Class cruisers, the two underwent considerable design revision to counter recently constructed French fast battleships that would outclass the smaller *Panzerschiffe*. After only five months of intermittent construction, the ships were cancelled and scrapped in favour of battleships *Scharnhorst* and *Gneisenau*. In 1940, the two surviving *Panzerschiffe* were officially reclassified as heavy cruisers. It was to the *Admiral Scheer* of this class that the accolade of most successful raiding voyage must be given after sinking 15 ships and capturing two others in 1940/41 within the Atlantic and Indian Oceans.

The stern half of the *Admiral Graf Spee*. The rangefinder for the stern battery is immediately behind the turret, the ship's aircraft just visible behind it. At the top of the superstructure is the primary rangefinder. (AC)

Heavy cruisers: *Admiral Hipper; Prinz Eugen* and *Blücher*

Despite being forbidden under Versailles Treaty terms to construct heavy cruisers, plans were drawn up during February 1934 for this class of vessel, capable of countering French equivalents and operating within the Atlantic Ocean. The decision was made to arm such a ship with eight 20cm (8in) SK/ C34 guns in four heavily armoured turrets, rather than a greater number of smaller calibre main guns. The secondary armament comprised 12 10.5cm SK C/33 anti-aircraft guns mounted in electrically stabilized twin turrets and controlled by the sophisticated stabilized flak fire control system with four 4m stereoscopic SL-6 'Basisgeräte' rangefinders. *Admiral Hipper* was provided at completion with a FuMo 22 radar.

The ships would be powered by high-pressure steam turbines, the overall configuration requiring a slight decrease in originally planned armour protection to keep it closer to Washington Treaty limitations for such a vessel. Orders for the first two – *Admiral Hipper* and *Blücher* – were placed in October 1934, though Germany still covertly denied breaking the Versailles Treaty limitations.

Hitler's dismissal of those limits in March 1935 lifted the veil of secrecy, the three ships still claiming to conform to the Anglo-German Naval Agreement's allowance of five 10,000-long-ton (10,160 ton) 'treaty cruisers', though they would far exceed that. During November, a third ship – *Prinz Eugen* – was ordered; slightly larger in length and beam than its predecessors. Two further ships never reached completion.

Admiral Hipper was commissioned on 29 April 1939 and steamed into the Baltic for trials. *Blücher* was commissioned on 20 September 1939 while *Prinz Eugen* did not enter Kriegsmarine service until 1 August 1940, its commissioning delayed after suffering damage in an RAF bombing raid on Kiel during July. By that date, *Blücher* was already gone; sunk in Drøbak Sound, the northernmost part of the outer Oslofjord in southern Norway, on 9 April 1940 as German

Heavy cruiser *Admiral Hipper*, commissioned in April 1939, its ambitious steam turbine propulsion plagued the ship with mechanical problems throughout its service. (AC)

forces began their invasion of Norway. The two remaining heavy cruisers would both see action in the Atlantic.

Both *Hipper* and *Prinz Eugen* were protected by upper deck armour ranging from 12 to 30mm, 20–50mm for the main deck. The ships' main belt was between 70 and 80mm, the main superstructure boasting armour that ranged from 50 to 150mm.

Though these cruisers carried advanced gunnery control systems, sights and radars, making them amongst the most potent heavy cruisers of their time on paper, they lacked range due to the lack of diesel engines which compromised their suitability for commerce raiding. Instead, the design emphasis had been on speed – specifically the ability to outpace the French *Dunkerque* battleships' highly sophisticated but overly complicated high-pressure turbines that proved unpredictable and unreliable in action. Constant mechanical problems hindered the operational use of both *Hipper* and *Prinz Eugen*; *Blücher* was not afloat long enough to demonstrate the same problems.

While both cruisers were capable of 32.5 knots, their range varied between 6,500nm at 17 knots for *Hipper* and only 5,050nm at 15 knots for *Prinz Eugen*. Compared to the 10,000nm at 20 knots that the *Deutschland*-class *Panzerschiff* could muster, the limitations for their employment as Atlantic raiders was obvious. More than ever, they relied on a strong tanker supporting force.

Light forces

The light cruisers of the German Navy played no active role within the Atlantic; *Emden*, *Karlsruhe*, *Köln*, *Königsberg*, *Leipzig* and *Nürnberg* fought their war within the North Sea and Baltic, and as such will be covered in separate volumes. However, the myriad smaller craft required for security duties around occupied France saw the location of several flotillas of patrol boats, minesweepers, submarine hunters and barrage breakers (*Sperrbrecher*) that were used to safeguard passages for larger ships and U-boats. These were indispensable to Kriegsmarine operations, though too numerous to list here.

Destroyers were among the first surface forces engaging the enemy within Atlantic waters as they waged war in the Western Approaches after relocating to France. Between 1940 and 1942 there were two destroyer flotillas stationed on the French Atlantic coast:

- *Zerstörerflottille* (Destroyer Flotilla) based in Brest from September to November 1940 when the flotilla comprised *Z4 Richard Beitzen*, *Z14 Freidrich Ihn*, *Z15 Erich Steinbrech* and *Z16 Freidrich Eckoldt*. In April 1941, the flotilla moved to La Pallice where it stayed until September, its composition: *Z8 Bruno Heinemann*, *Z14*, *Z15*, *Z23* and *Z24*.
- *Zerstörerflottille* which operated from Brest between September and November 1940, comprised *Z5 Paul Jacobi*, *Z6 Theodore Riedel*, *Z10 Hans Lody* and *Z20 Karl Galster*.

The initial duty of these flotillas in 1940 was an extension of their North Sea role and the laying of mines along the English coastlines. *Z16 Friedrich Eckoldt* covered five other destroyers laying mines in Falmouth Bay during the night of 28/29 September. Five ships totalling only 2,026 GRT were sunk by this minefield. Then, in 1941, the emphasis placed upon *5. Zerstörerflottille* was the escort of surface ships along the French edge of the Bay of Biscay.

German naval torpedo boats of World War II were essentially small destroyers, though the etymology can lead to confusion with S-boats – 'E-boats' in English literature – which were equivalent to MTBs. Torpedo boats displaced less than 1,000 tons, until the Type 39 variant when they began to resemble their larger counterparts and were being designed with operations within the North Atlantic in mind. This distinction between the two had its origins in the pre-World War I Imperial German Navy and continued until 1945. It is a widely held belief that although the German vessels of both types were comparatively heavily armed with large cannon, their seagoing qualities were inferior to that of their Allied counterparts, probably due to being top-heavy with large weaponry aboard the slim hull.

Although both types of vessels were essentially destroyers, the German command structure initially made a definite distinction between the two. All German destroyers were under the command of the *Führer der Zerstörer* (F.d.Z. or Destroyer Leader) – six men occupied this post before the war's end; whilst the torpedo boats came under the control of *Führer der Torpedoboote* (F.d.T. or Torpedo Boats Leader) – *Kapitän zur See* Hans Bütow from 30 September 1939 to the post's dissolution on 20 April 1942 when torpedo boats were transferred to F.d.Z. control. Both high commands were placed directly beneath the B.d.A. (*Befehlshaber der Aufklärungsstreitkräfte*) command umbrella, and those operating from French bases answered to MGK West (*Marinegruppenkommando West*).

On the French Atlantic coast there were also three torpedo boat flotillas stationed at various times between 1940 and the end of 1942. Their deployment makes dizzying reading and is not listed here in full, though the basic locations and orders of battle were:

- *Torpedobootsflottille*, based initially in Cherbourg from September 1940 to November 1941 but spread between Brest and La Pallice from the date of Operation *Cerberus* numbering a total of 12 torpedo boats in total.
- *Torpedobootsflottille*, of nine ships originally stationed in Dunkirk in February 1942, then spread between the north coast of Brittany and La Pallice between July and December.
- *Torpedobootsflottille*, again spread between the north of Brittany and La Pallice between September 1940 and July 1944. The ships were the oldest torpedo boats of the Kriegsmarine: *Falke*, *Greif*, *Kondor* and *Möwe* were augmented in February 1941 with *Iltis*, *Jaguar* and *Seeadler*.

Among the defensive vessels operating along the Atlantic coast under MGK West's control, minesweepers were perhaps the most common. Though flotillas of M35-class purpose-built minesweepers were deployed, the majority remained converted trawlers. The M35 class was developed from proven World War I vessels; displacing over 870 tons and carrying heavy armaments for a minesweeper (with two 10.5cm cannon, one 3.7cm and two 2cm flak weapons) enabled them to sometimes tangle with enemy destroyer units within the English Channel. Multi-purposed, they could be fitted for minelaying and were able to carry 30 mines on hull rails as well as four depth-charge launchers for ASW (anti-submarine warfare) work. They were constructed in three different series: Type 1935, ordered between 1935 and 1936; Type 1938, with increased hull dimensions providing better sea-keeping qualities and allowing for the installation of additional generators for magnetic sweeps; Type 1939 (Mob), which had been ordered after the outbreak of war with emphasis on simplified construction.

Converted trawlers were commonly used as minesweepers, patrol boats (*Vorpostenboote*) and submarine hunters (*U-Boot Jäger*) within Biscay; often the divisions between the three vessel types and their tasks blurred as the vessels shared a basic structural commonality. As in 1914, at the outbreak of World War II, most of Germany's ocean-going trawlers had been commandeered by the Kriegsmarine and converted to military use. Additionally, dozens of fishing vessels from conquered countries were also impressed into service. Flotilla composition varied widely, as did ship configuration, but typically they began the war with a single 7.5cm or 8.8cm World War I vintage naval cannon, recalibrated to fire newer ammunition, as well as a single 2cm C/30 with additional lighter machine-gun mountings, and the depth charges. Many Security Force vessels, particularly *U-Boot Jäger*, also carried *S-Gerät* sonar equipment coupled with KDB hydrophone gear for the detection of enemy submarines.

One further class of vessel found in French Atlantic waters was the *Sperrbrecher* (barrage breakers) designed to combat enemy mines. During 1937 the Kriegsmarine began converting requisitioned cargo vessels to *Sperrbrecher* and eventually a shortlist of 58 merchants was established that ranged from the 3,164-ton MV *Henry Horn* of Hamburg's H. C. Horn Shipping Line, to 9,626-ton freighter and passenger liner SS *Königstein* of Arnold Bernstein's shipping company.

The shipboard Arado Ar196 floatplane launches from *Admiral Hipper*. All such aircrew were assigned to the Luftwaffe's *Bordfliegerstaffel* 1./Bo.Fl. Gr.196, a catch-all squadron from which shipborne aircraft and crews were drawn. They provided valuable reconnaissance services both hunting for convoys and evading enemy naval forces. (Naval Heritage and History Command)

In general, a *Sperrbrecher* complement was approximately 85 men; a mixture of World War I veteran reservists, merchant seamen and young recruits. They carried a variety of minesweeping gear that evolved as the war progressed, though there was also a default method of minesweeping for the deep draught *Sperrbrecher*. To enable a brute force approach, the holds were filled with buoyant material – a so-called 'protective cargo' – above a shock-absorbent layer of sand and, if all else failed, the *Sperrbrecher* would detonate mines by sailing into them and simply absorbing the punishment while hopefully remaining afloat.

Sperrbrecher were initially armed with a single 10.5cm C/96 cannon mounted aft and two 2cm C/30 cannon either forward or near the bridge, though as the war progressed and Allied air power increased, so too did their flak weaponry. Eventually they were so heavily armed that the RAF knew them as 'heavy flak ships'. The role of the *Sperrbrecher* was defined in instructions issued during April 1938, including mine defence, merchant convoy escort, reporting of enemy aircraft and anti-submarine duties; all of which was controlled by the regional *Führer der Minensuchboote*.

GUNNERY AND FIRE CONTROL

Naval guns designed between 1920 and 1940 were designated by their bore diameter (in centimetres), 'SK' meaning *Schiffskanone* (ship's cannon) followed by the construction year. For example, the main guns aboard *Scharnhorst* were 28cm SK C/34; 28cm bore (11in) constructed in 1934. This replaced the previous designation that was identical except the construction year was omitted in favour of the nominal barrel length expressed as calibre (e.g. the pre-dreadnought *Schleswig Holstein*'s main guns were 28cm SK L/40). As in the previous war, the weak point of most German capital ships was their relatively small main gun calibre.

During 1934 the GEMA firm (*Gesellschaft für elektroakustische und mechanische Apparate*) built the first commercial radar continuous wave

Forward guns of *Admiral Graf Spee*; three 28cm (11in) SK C/28 guns, capable of outgunning most contemporary heavy cruisers. The protrusions that are on either side at the rear of the triple turret house are the back-up optical rangefinder. (Naval Heritage and History Command)

system for detecting ships, ostensibly for use as an anti-collision system. Operating on a 50cm wavelength (500MHz), it could detect the general area in which ships were located up to 10km distant. Further development at the Kriegsmarine's behest yielded a pulse radar in the summer of 1935 that in tests could locate the cruiser *Königsberg* at a distance of 8km, with a margin of error of only 50m. The same system could also detect an aircraft at 500m altitude up to 28km away. The nautical application of this was named *Seetakt FuMO* (*Funkmess-Ortung* – radio direction finder). This original *Seetakt* model proved troublesome and was improved to operate at the 60cm (500MHz) wavelength; an initial unit was installed on the *Admiral Graf Spee* in January 1938, followed by units aboard light cruiser *Königsberg*, the torpedo boat G10 and the communications test ship *Strahl*. Later production models operated over the range of 82–77cm (368–390 MHz) with a maximum range against a ship-sized target at sea of up to 220km in optimal conditions. In 1941, the updated FuMO 21 was introduced. The aerial was a 2m by 6m 'mattress' construction attached to the ships' foretop rangefinder.

German destroyers sailing line ahead into action. Present briefly on the French Atlantic coast, German destroyers were not as seaworthy as some of their British counterparts, probably due to being heavily armed and therefore top heavy with a slim hull. Nevertheless, they periodically appeared in action on the Atlantic fringe. (Piemags/Alamy Stock Photo)

Somewhat ironically given what followed during the war years, German radar development at first outpaced the British; the *Seetakt* in service before any British warships possessed an operational radar. However, the perennial disorganization and lack of focused direction from higher commands that plagued German wartime production in all military branches served to stunt further radar development. The Kriegsmarine regarded radar as a low priority and, as *Seetakt* was considered not accurate enough to use for direct gun laying, continued to concentrate on optical fire control using the superb Zeiss stereoscopic rangefinders.

In general, German gunnery was excellent. In exercises aboard *Bismarck*, the customary method of attack was to open fire with three partial salvoes in rapid succession, set at different ranges, so that all three were in the air at the same time. After observing the fall of shot, corrections would be made by the Artillery Officer and usually the second salvo group would be straddling the target. Once the correct range was found, full salvoes from all eight guns would begin.

Also, beginning with the *Admiral Hipper* and also installed on *Prinz Eugen*, *Bismarck*, *Scharnhorst* and *Gneisenau*, among other ships, was a sophisticated stabilized flak fire control system with four 4m stereoscopic SL-6 (upgraded on *Bismarck* to SL-8) *Basisgeräte* rangefinders crowned by their distinctive spherical covers. These controlled the heavy 10.5cm flak batteries and, because the rangefinders were electro-hydraulically stabilized and automatically changed their orientation in reaction to the motion of the ship, they were nicknamed by the crews *Wackeltopf*, meaning 'Chinese wok' but literally translated as 'wobbly pot'.

HOW THE FLEET OPERATED

NAVAL COMMAND

To understand the role played by Naval Group West (*Marinegruppenkommando West*) in surface operations, it is essential to look at the Kriegsmarine's organizational structure which remained in a near-constant state of evolution throughout the war, though the scope of this study concentrates on the years 1939 to 1942.

On 1 June 1935 German naval command was renamed from *Marineleitung* to *Oberkommando der Kriegsmarine* (OKM). Kriegsmarine command occupied offices within the Bendlerblock on the Tirpitzufer facing Berlin's Landwehr Canal. *Grossadmiral* Erich Raeder occupied the position of Commander-in-Chief of the Navy (*Oberbefehlshaber der Kriegsmarine*) and as such headed OKM. Immediately below Raeder's office, the Naval War Command was formed in 1937 by the amalgamation of previous positions; this *Seekriegsleitung*, shortened to SKL, was essentially a combined Planning and Operations Department for the Kriegsmarine which also included the Intelligence Division. By the outbreak of war, *Admiral* Otto Schniewind occupied the post of Chief of Staff of SKL.

It was SKL who were in direct control of surface forces tasked with attacking the enemy's supply lines within the Atlantic, including whatever supporting tankers and supply ships were required to enable such raiders. Though U-boats received direction from both SKL and MGK, they remained under the direct command of *Führer der Unterseeboote* (FdU) Karl Dönitz (his post soon redesignated *Befehlshaber der Unterseeboote* (BdU)) while MGK West and East were responsible solely for surface craft operating within the North Sea and Baltic respectively. This changed with the fall of France in June 1940 and relocation of Naval Group West from Wilhelmshaven to Paris with the subsequent extension of its authority and operational jurisdiction.

Progress in radio communications through cooperation between the Reichsmarine and private Telefunken Company had yielded an efficient and compact radio set that was used aboard light coastal forces such as minesweepers and S-boats. From 1932, naval radio messages were transmitted to cooperative merchant ships that in turn relayed them to military vessels further afield, an imperfect system at best. Raeder understood that future naval operations would be coordinated and directed by shore-based headquarters; the role into which the Naval Group Commands were inserted.

Naval Group West (*Marinegruppenkommando West*)

The Naval Group Commands controlled all Kriegsmarine forces within their geographical sphere of operations, which included security forces such as patrol boats, minesweepers of all types and submarine hunters that were used to safeguard German convoy traffic and the coastal approaches to ports and harbours. Responsibility for the collation and dissemination of intelligence information supplied by Luftwaffe maritime units or the B-Dienst radio listening service to all their assigned vessels at sea was also given to the Naval Group Commands. While MGK East had been established in October 1938, MGK West only came into being in August 1939, command given to *Admiral* Alfred Saalwächter, an experienced officer who had entered the Imperial Navy in 1910 and whose subsequent experience included two years as a U-boat commander during the previous war.

Saalwächter's Chief of Staff was *Kapitän zur See* Paul Wever for the first months of war, replaced in December 1939 by *Konteradmiral* Otto Ciliax, former commander of *Scharnhorst*, as Wever transferred to SKL as Chief of the Department for Naval Intelligence Analysis (3/SKL). Originally, Naval Group

Generaladmiral Alfred Saalwächter, chief of Naval Group West between August 1939 and September 1942. Naval Group West controlled Atlantic surface operations, except for the disguised merchant raiders. He resigned from active service in November 1942. After the war, Saalwächter was imprisoned by the Soviet Union, convicted of war crimes and executed by firing squad in Moscow on 6 December 1945. Following the dissolution of the Soviet Union, Saalwächter was formally exonerated by a Russian court. (History and Art Collection/Alamy Stock Photo)

West comprised four departments headed by Staff Officers (*Admiralstabsoffizier*) – a number later expanded to six – and an Engineering Officer. The original four departments were:

1. *Admiralstabsoffizier* (A1 or Asto 1) *Kapitän zur See* Hans Meyer (operations)
2. *Admiralstabsoffizier* (A2) *Korvettenkapitän* Werner Pfeiffer (inbound and outbound routing)
3. *Admiralstabsoffizier* (A3) *Kapitänleutnant* Karl Adolf Zenker (reconnaissance)
4. *Admiralstabsoffizier* (A4) *Kapitän zur See* Heinz Bonatz (intelligence and communications)

A Quartermaster Staff was added in November 1942.

Previous to the establishment of the Naval Group Commands, the Fleet Commander (*Flottenchef*), *Admiral* Hermann Boehm had operated independently immediately below the SKL level. However, the insertion of MGK West between these two hierarchical levels allowed a more cohesive operational planning structure to be put into place.

Putting control of the forces at sea under appropriate commands ashore provided for transmitting all possible information to the units at sea, as well as all directives and orders without these units having to ask. These forces would have the confident feeling that they were getting their orders from an authority which, through continuous, close association, was thoroughly familiar with their problems – a confidence that was increased by the feeling that they were being left to make decisions from their own on-the-spot observations and at their own discretion.[6]

During the early days of the war, while *Admiral Graf Spee* and *Deutschland* were in their waiting positions before being granted operational freedom, Naval Group West remained concerned solely with the North Sea operations as it hadn't yet been given responsibility for the Atlantic theatre. Saalwächter's part played in the departure of those two ships had been limited to responsibility for escorting forces and supplying up-to-date intelligence while they headed towards the North Atlantic.

During September 1939 Saalwächter informed SKL that major surface operations within the North Sea were inadvisable, both due to a lack of available destroyers and the fact that heavy units *Scharnhorst* and *Gneisenau* were still engaged in working-up exercises within the Baltic Sea. In Berlin, SKL was in full agreement with Saalwächter and issued memorandum that cemented the issue of naval control within the North Sea area, firmly instructing that 'all offensive warfare and the operational use of Fleet forces, even in the Skagerrak and Kattegat, must remain the task of Commanding Admiral, Naval Group West, and thus be subject to one single authority.'[7]

---

6   Raeder, Erich, *Grand Admiral*, De Capo, 2001, p. 297.
7   SKL War Diary, 18 September 1939.

This new arrangement was not, however, without its complications as initial friction developed between the Naval Group West and the Fleet Commander over where final authority lay. Somewhat surprisingly, however, cooperation between Saalwächter's Naval Group West and the Luftwaffe's F.d.Luft West (Joachim Coeler), Felmy's Luftflotte 2 and Geisler's 10. *Fliegerdivision* was initially very positive. Despite the fact that the Luftwaffe and Kriegsmarine had failed to coordinate the most basic tenets of cohesive maritime war – each used different map grids, there was no established mutual communications net, no common code or cypher system, inadequate telecommunications between operational headquarters and command stations – an element of goodwill had been fostered, not least of all due to Coeler's obvious enthusiasm for his aircraft to begin maritime operations. Overcoming the difficulties imposed by the joint control of naval air units, local organizational measures were taken between the various headquarters: Saalwächter based in Wilhelmshaven, Coeler in Yever 21km to the west, Felmy in Braunschweig and Geisler's office located in Hamburg which boasted a highly developed signals net. The Luftwaffe and Naval offices immediately exchanged grid-square charts, enabling a composite overlay to be created to ease operational coordination. Communications systems were rapidly improved upon and a Luftwaffe liaison officer, *Oberst* Hans Metzner, was quickly assigned to Saalwächter's staff.

Pocket battleships *Admiral Graf Spee* and *Deutschland* putting to sea before the beginning of the war. Both ships carried eight torpedo tubes mounted towards the stern. (AC)

FLEET COMMAND (*FLOTTENKOMMANDO*)

Hierarchically immediately below the Naval Group lay the Fleet Command, headed at the outbreak of war by *Flottenchef Admiral* Hermann Boehm until his resignation in October 1939. At that time the new battleship *Gneisenau* served as Boehm's flagship of the fleet. The position of *Flottenchef* was essentially administrative in nature; the fleet commander was not necessarily in direct control of a fleet at sea but rather the senior officer to which all major surface ship commanders reported.

However, jurisdictional conflict between a succession of Fleet Commanders and Naval Group West did not abate until July 1940. The original contentious issue revolved around the use of minelaying destroyers within the North Sea. While Boehm wanted to use heavy units to support destroyers on their way back to German waters after each mission, Saalwächter instead ordered mining carried out under cover of winter darkness without the application of valuable and scarce heavy ships and with cover for the minelayers' withdrawal provided by Luftwaffe maritime aircraft. The matter became so acrimonious that, after SKL ruled in favour of MGK West rather than the Fleet Command, Boehm resigned his post. Nonetheless, Boehm's replacement, *Admiral* Wilhelm Marschall as well as *Vizeadmiral* Gunther Lütjens (B.d.A.) remained unhappy about this new command arrangement which they felt robbed them of a certain autonomy as commander on the spot.

It was, perhaps predictably, Marschall's undoing as well since he exercised what he believed to be the Fleet Commander's prerogative during the last phase of the German invasion of Norway and ignored his original orders in Operation *Juno* to interrupt resupply efforts for Allied troops in Norway. Encountering retreating British naval forces, Marschall attacked. Despite sinking the carrier HMS *Glorious* and escorting destroyers *Ardent* and *Acasta*, *Scharnhorst* was damaged by a torpedo fired by the latter killing 48 men and causing severe damage. Marschall wrote directly to Raeder on 28 June to explain his actions and disagreement with the division of command between Fleet Commander and MGK West. He ended his five pages with the words, 'As fleet commander, I have a duty to express my opinion to the commander-in-chief who was most recently responsible – especially when their views seem to diverge or there is a risk that people are talking past each other. If the decision is made, I, like every other officer in the fleet, will be a soldier and will obey.'

Nonetheless, his failure to follow strict MGK West orders resulted in Raeder replacing Marschall with Günther Lütjens in July 1940 on the grounds that Marschall's health rendered him no longer up to the task.[8] Aware of his two predecessors' fates, Lütjens became determined to follow his orders to the letter: perhaps to the potential detriment of future operations.

At the time of Lütjens' promotion to Fleet Commander, *Gneisenau* was superseded as flagship by *Bismarck*; the *Admiral* later putting to sea aboard this ship on its ill-fated maiden voyage and assuming tactical command during the Battle of the Denmark Strait. Lütjens was killed when *Bismarck* sank, making him the sole Fleet Commander to die in combat.

With the addition of the Naval Group to command hierarchy, the role of Fleet Commander became far more advisory than any of the men who held the post wanted and the acrimonious relationship that had begun with Boehm and Saalwächter continued with each successive officer appointee until organizational changes were attempted in 1943 by which time the era of the Atlantic raiders was over.

Günther Lütjens, described as one of the ablest officers in the Kriegsmarine. Though austere and frequently considered aloof, he rose to Fleet Commander in July 1940 and would lead the successful joint operation between *Scharnhorst* and *Gneisenau* (his flagship). He appears to have been negative regarding the potential success of *Bismarck*'s inaugural mission and was killed aboard the ship in May 1941. (Interfoto/Alamy Stock Photo)

Fleet Commanders

Adm. Hermann Boehm: November 1938–October 1939

Adm. Wilhelm Marschall: October 1939–July 1940

Adm. Günther Lütjens: July 1940–27 May 1941 (killed in action with his entire staff)

Genadm. Otto Schniewind: June 1941–July 1944

Vizeadm. Wilhelm Meensden-Bohlken: July 1944–May 1945

Beneath Fleet Command, a somewhat bewildering array of offices had been created and either dissolved or amalgamated in the years preceding war. By September 1939 the Commander-in-Chief of *Panzerschiffe* (*Befehlshaber der Panzerschiffe*, or B.d.P.) controlled all battleships and pocket battleships: *Scharnhorst*, *Gneisenau*, *Admiral Graf Spee*, *Admiral Scheer* and *Deutschland*. At that time, it was *Vizeadmiral* Wilhelm Marschall who occupied the post, his flagship the *Admiral Graf Spee*. Cruisers were the domain of Commander-in-Chief Reconnaissance Forces (B.d.A.), *Vizeadmiral* Hermann Densch in command until October 1939 whereupon he handed over command to Lütjens. The ships *Admiral Hipper*, *Nürnberg* (Densch's flagship), *Leipzig* and *Köln* were his responsibility. Subordinate to B.d.A. was the Leader of Torpedo Boats (*Führer der Torpedoboote*, or F.d.T.) who held responsibility for all destroyers, torpedo boats and S-boats. Minesweepers of all types were the domain of the Leader of Minesweepers (*Führer der Minensuchboote*, or F.d.M.) *Kapitän zur See* Friedrich Ruge, a torpedo boat veteran of World

---

8 Somewhat ironically, Wilhelm Marschall would later become the commander of MGK West in September 1942.

MGK WEST INSTALLATIONS IN FRANCE, JANUARY 1942

In June 1940 the office of *Kommandierender Admiral Frankreich* had been established in the ex-French Naval Ministry on Place de la Concorde, Paris, to control naval deployments within France and Belgium. *Marinegruppenkommando West*, previously operating from Sengwarden near Wilhelmshaven, transferred to Paris during August 1940 and the *Kommandierender Admiral Frankreich* post continued to operate as a sub-unit until November 1943 when it was disbanded.

The Channel coast had been initially subdivided into two separate commands before 1941 when *Admiral* Hermann von Fischel was named overall commander of the entire region stretching from the Belgian border to St Malo.

In June, *Kapitän zur See* Robin Schall-Ernden was named overall commander of the Kriegsmarine in Western France outside of Brittany (*Marinebefehlshaber Westfrankreich*; later the title modified to *Marinebefehlshaber Atlantikküste*), with headquarters in Royan, near Bordeaux. In December 1940, it was enlarged to include Brittany.

Coinciding with the reorganization of France's Kriegsmarine command, various structural enhancements were made to the naval region. Three sub-sectors were created covering all land-based naval personnel of the Kriegsmarine's Atlantic coast. Stretching along France's Atlantic coast, there were three districts: *Seeko Bretagne*, *Seeko Loire* and *Seeko Gascogne*. These naval districts each had their own commander designated *Seekommandant* (*Seeko*, translated as Flag Officer of naval district).

Beneath the umbrella of each *Seeko* was a range of sub-commands catering to the needs of the occupying navy:

Hafenkommandant and *Hafenkapitän* (Hako and Haka)	Port commandant and captains respectively, responsible for all port operations with attached company of marines – the former holding greater authority than the latter.
Kriegsmarinearsenal	Naval arms depots
Kriegsmarinedienststelle	Personnel services
Marine Artillerie Abteilungen	Coastal artillery, both heavy and light
Marine Flak Artillerie Abteilungen	Naval flak artillery
Hafenschutzflotillen	Harbour patrol boats – small lightly armed fishing boats
Marine Kraftfahr Abteilungen	Naval transport units
Marine Funkmess Abteilungen	Naval radio detection units
Marine Nebel Abteilungen	Smoke laying units

Units of *Netzsperrflotille West* provided ports with protection from submarine attack. Anchored in place and suspended from large buoys, thick steel mesh anti-submarine nets stretched across port entrance channels, moved aside by steam tugboats to allow vessels free transit to the open sea.

Naval shipbuilding

Outside of *Seeko* control, five *Kriegsmarinewerft* (KMW), or naval shipbuilders, were established at Brest (A), Lorient (B), St Nazaire (C), La Pallice (D, the port of La Rochelle) and Bordeaux (E). In Brest it was the Deschimag company of Bremen that began construction of vessels and marine engines in November 1940 within the old French Arsenal. *Korvettenkapitan* August Vollheim took initial command of this unit that eventually incorporated several varied construction services, torpedo supply and repair and personnel services.

Security units

VA Friedrich Ruge's office of *Befehlshaber der Sicherung West* controlled all forms of minesweeper or mine clearance ships, patrol boats, submarine hunters and artillery carrier units. This office had been undergoing substantial changes since 1940. By January 1942, four *Sicherungsdivisionen* had been created:

1st Sicherungsdivision was responsible for the Netherlands and Germany's North Sea coast

2nd Sicherungsdivision was based near Boulogne

3rd Sicherungsdivision was based initially at Brest before moving to Trez Hir near Plougenvelin

4th Sicherungsdivision was based at Larmor-Plage near Lorient.

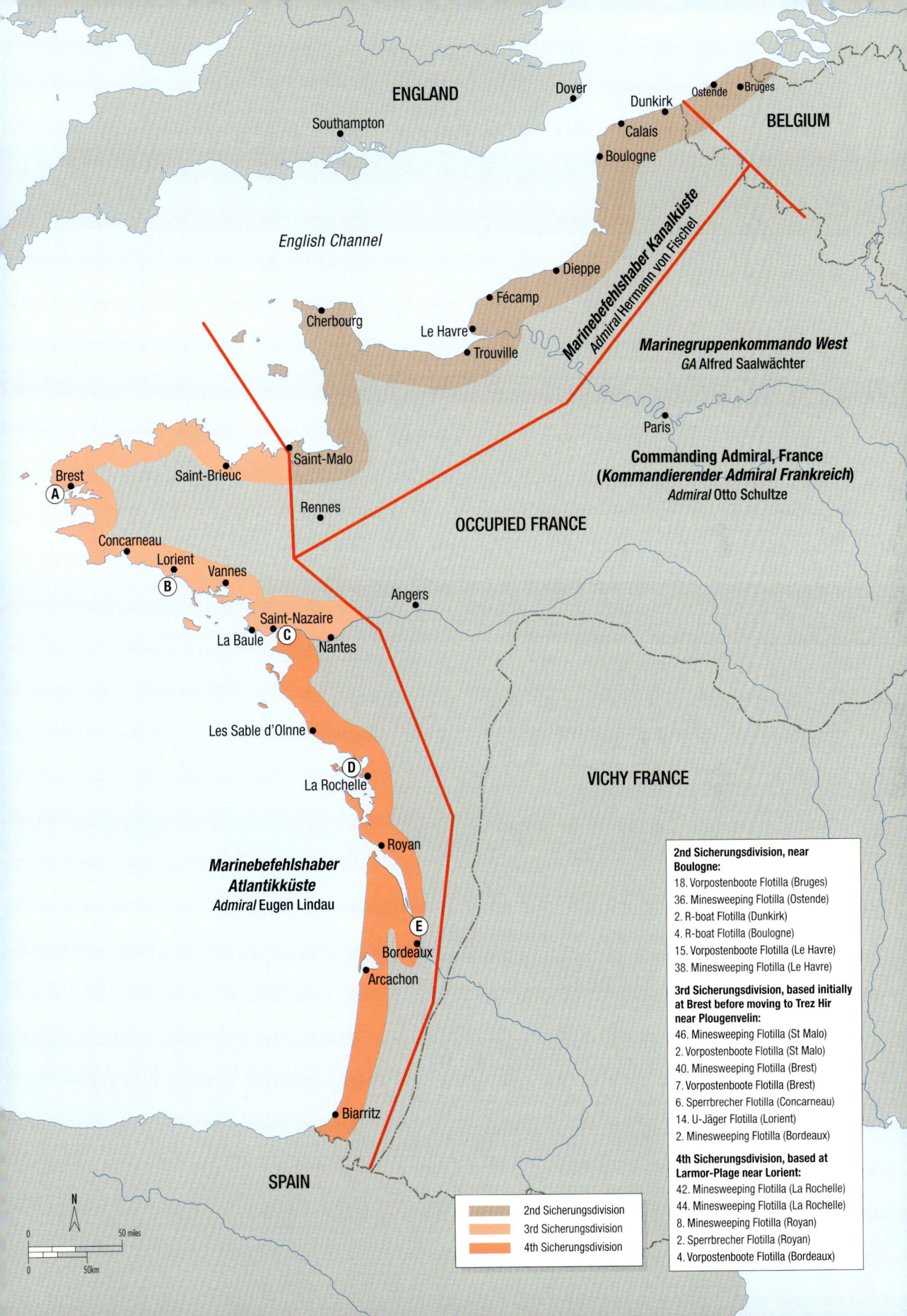

ENGLAND

Southampton

Dover

Dunkirk

Ostende   Bruges

BELGIUM

Calais

Boulogne

English Channel

Dieppe

Fécamp

Cherbourg

Le Havre

Trouville

Marinebefehlshaber Kanalküste
Admiral Hermann von Fischel

Marinegruppenkommando West
GA Alfred Saalwächter

Paris

Saint-Malo

A Brest

Saint-Brieuc

Rennes

Commanding Admiral, France
(***Kommandierender Admiral Frankreich***)
Admiral Otto Schultze

OCCUPIED FRANCE

Concarneau

Lorient

Vannes

B

Angers

Saint-Nazaire

C

La Baule   Nantes

Les Sable d'Olnne

D

La Rochelle

VICHY FRANCE

Royan

*Marinebefehlshaber
Atlantikküste*
Admiral Eugen Lindau

E

Bordeaux

Arcachon

Biarritz

SPAIN

N

0   50 miles

0   50km

2nd Sicherungsdivision

3rd Sicherungsdivision

4th Sicherungsdivision

**2nd Sicherungsdivision, near
Boulogne:**

18. Vorpostenboote Flotilla (Bruges)

36. Minesweeping Flotilla (Ostende)

2. R-boat Flotilla (Dunkirk)

4. R-boat Flotilla (Boulogne)

15. Vorpostenboote Flotilla (Le Havre)

38. Minesweeping Flotilla (Le Havre)

**3rd Sicherungsdivision, based initially
at Brest before moving to Trez Hir
near Plougenvelin:**

46. Minesweeping Flotilla (St Malo)

2. Vorpostenboote Flotilla (St Malo)

40. Minesweeping Flotilla (Brest)

7. Vorpostenboote Flotilla (Brest)

6. Sperrbrecher Flotilla (Concarneau)

14. U-Jäger Flotilla (Lorient)

2. Minesweeping Flotilla (Bordeaux)

**4th Sicherungsdivision, based at
Larmor-Plage near Lorient:**

42. Minesweeping Flotilla (La Rochelle)

44. Minesweeping Flotilla (La Rochelle)

8. Minesweeping Flotilla (Royan)

2. Sperrbrecher Flotilla (Royan)

4. Vorpostenboote Flotilla (Bordeaux)

War I, his office only removed from B.d.A. authority shortly before the outbreak of war.

Naval Group West and the move to France

After the successful German invasion, the official end of active fighting in France came with an armistice, signed on 22 June 1940. Despite isolated areas not fully submitting for several weeks, hostilities were over as of 0135hrs on 25 June and German occupation began immediately. A partitioning line was established that allowed south-eastern France nominal self-government under *Maréchal* Pétain's newly established Vichy regime.

The potential of existing French Navy bases at Brest and Lorient as forward staging areas for the Kriegsmarine, particularly the U-boat arm, was obvious, and surveys immediately made of their condition. Many vessels had been scuttled in the ports during the chaotic Anglo-French retreat, and a large number raised either to clear channels, for scrap, or for rehabilitation as part of the Kriegsmarine. In addition to the two existing French military bases, the industrial and commercial ports at St Nazaire, La Pallice (within the city of La Rochelle) and Bordeaux were judged suitable for expansion as Kriegsmarine bases, and equipment convoys were soon rumbling from Germany along roads still littered with the rubble of blitzkrieg.

However, requests on 23 June by Saalwächter to relocate to France and control the Atlantic war was denied by SKL. In Berlin, great tasks were still expected in the North Sea and northern waters off Norway, and with no surface forces yet available for Atlantic operations, MGK West's presence in France was considered unnecessary. It was not until Saalwächter was given responsibility for planning the abortive Operation *Sealion* invasion of Britain that the matter was again discussed in Berlin. At that point, the decision was made that MGK West's operational area would have to be completely refocused in support of its main task. To that end, MGK West was considered best transferred to wherever cooperation with the Army Group earmarked for the invasion was best achieved to ensure proper communications and command channels between all commands involved, particularly between SKL and the Group. The transfer of Naval Staff to the vicinity of Führer Headquarters was prepared while a new Naval Group North would take over the previous tasks of MGK West and MGK East. For the planning and execution of *Sealion*, MGK West transferred to France where Commanding Admiral, Naval Forces, West; Commanding Admiral, Defences, West; Commander, Minesweepers, West; and Air Commander, West were all to be subordinated to Saalwächter. Before long, *Sealion* was postponed indefinitely.

MGK West relocated from Sengwarden to Paris and the ex-French Navy Ministry building on Place de la Concorde during August 1940 to take direct command of all Kriegsmarine units within France and Belgium. Coupled with this enlarged sphere of responsibility that included the entire coastline from the Netherlands border with Belgium to the Franco-Spanish border, all Atlantic surface operations were placed under its control. Any ships departing Germany were now under orders from Naval Group North under *Generaladmiral* Rolf Carls, situated in Saalwächter's former Sengwarden offices, until they reached the line stretching from southern Greenland to the Northern Hebrides whereupon they passed into Saalwächter's control. Luftwaffe maritime units and U-boats remained operationally independent, though duty bound to honour deployment requests by Naval Groups.

Such defensive craft as minesweepers, submarine hunters and patrol boats soon became the domain of the *Sicherungsdivisionen* (Security Divisions); comprised of several flotillas, each with a specified purpose. With the German sphere of influence expanded enormously, and in need of protection, the Kriegsmarine established on 27 October 1940 the office of *Befehlshaber der Sicherung West* (Commander of Western Security) alongside similar offices for other occupied territories. Initially this new command post was held by *Vizeadmiral* Hermann Moontz (the first of four wartime commanders) whose headquarters was located in Trouville, near Le Havre. It was beneath the umbrella of *Befehlshaber der Sicherung West* that two distinct branches operated: *Führer der Minensuchverbände West* (Commander of Western Minesweepers) and *Führer der Vorpostenverbände West* (Commander Western Patrol Boats). The former post was occupied by Ruge, while the latter office belonged to *Kapitän zur See* Heinz Schiller.

There followed an almost constant reshuffling and fine-tuning of the often ponderous command structures and control boundaries. During January 1941 Moontz departed as *Befehlshaber der Sicherung West* to be briefly replaced by *Vizeadmiral* Hermann von Fischel. Finally in April 1941 the two separate offices of Coastal Defence and Minesweeper Commands were amalgamated and placed under the sole command of *Befehlshaber der Sicherung West* – held from 17 February 1941 by newly promoted and extremely able *Vizeadmiral* Friedrich Ruge – and transferred to the Western headquarters building in Paris. These were the little ships that dominated German Atlantic coastal operations.

OPERATIONAL DOCTRINE

During the inter-war period, wargames and theoretical studies were carried out within the Reichsmarine as new fast light cruisers entered service and the development of 'pocket battleships' became a reality. The tactical possibilities offered by the increased speed and flexibility of major surface units led to the development of the 'task force' concept as the mainstay of Kriegsmarine operations. The previous war's doctrine of massed fleet deployment had proved relatively futile and had now been outmoded by the introduction of naval air power. Instead, the Kriegsmarine adopted the Task Force or, *Kampfgruppe* (Battle Group) concept; assembling a single unit of various ship types in order to accomplish any given objective. This Task Force would then be placed under

Admiral Hipper practising refuelling in the North Sea. The Germans used the line-astern method for refuelling as opposed to the line-abreast method used by the US Navy, the latter considered more efficient though more difficult to master. (AC)

broad control of the Naval Groups while retaining some ability for the Force commander to act independently to achieve his stated aim.

By this rationale there was no firm subdivision of the battleships and cruisers of the High Seas Fleet into squadrons; each craft available for whatever task was at hand. The remaining smaller ship classes were grouped into traditional flotillas, geographically posted with considerable flexibility wherever they were required.

AN OPTIMAL CONVOY ATTACK USING SURFACE RAIDERS, U-BOATS AND LUFTWAFFE AIRCRAFT

Cooperation between Luftwaffe maritime units, major surface ships and U-boats had been a long-cherished idea held particularly by Karl Dönitz, the head of the U-boat arm. Both he and Raeder had bemoaned the inability to form a dedicated naval air arm in the face of continual resistance from Hermann Göring, the vainglorious chief of the Luftwaffe. Nevertheless, the Luftwaffe did create a number of dedicated maritime strike/reconnaissance squadrons. In the Atlantic, KG 40 was the most important of these, operating predominantly the Focke Wulf Fw200 'Condor' aircraft; a sleek though flawed design.

Given the perfect opportunity, the combination of these three units would proceed along these lines:

1. The Luftwaffe aircraft would locate enemy convoy traffic and signal its coordinates to MGK West and BdU. The aircraft wouldn't immediately attack, being more valuable in shadowing and reporting the convoy's track and location.

2. As long as no enemy capital ships were present, any available heavy surface units in range would close in on the convoy and engage its destroyer escorts with superior weaponry; they would be able to keep out of range as the escort ships were eliminated as a potential threat.

3. U-boats would then proceed to attack the scattering merchant ships which were now bereft of escort. Any KG 40 aircraft still on station would also attack.

In practice this strategy never worked; the sole example of it coming close was the cooperation between *Admiral Hipper*, U37 and KG 40 aircraft in February 1941 against convoy HG53 (which led to the successful attack on SLS64). In general, attempts to coordinate such efforts were frustrated by a lack of available units, poor Luftwaffe navigational fixes for naval use and a frequent unwillingness of Luftwaffe crews to shadow a convoy instead of attacking it.

Convoy

1
Luftwaffe KG 40 conducts reconnaissance

2
Surface ship engages and destroys convoy escort

3
U-boats attack scattered merchantmen

The concept by which Raeder had begun amassing his surface fleet was nullified by the premature outbreak of war. Rather than combat against enemy naval forces, they were instead to practice mercantile warfare aimed at the destruction of Britain's Atlantic supply lines. By using rapidly moving raiders within the North and South Atlantic, Raeder hoped to combine the effects of dislocation of convoy traffic, sinking of enemy merchant ships, and the tying down of significant British and French naval units in chasing these ships which would relocate frequently and quickly to confuse the enemy as to their location. The act of disguising a ship to resemble others would also be used to sow further confusion.

However, due to both the limited number of such ships available and the paranoia that permeated Hitler's thinking as supreme military commander of all Germany's armed forces, the captains of all major warships were repeatedly told to take 'no unnecessary risks'. This amounted to instructions that the appearance of enemy naval forces was enough reason to disengage from any convoy action; leading to a resultant inability to press home an aggressive attack. In essence, the Nelsonian naval tradition of 'engaging the enemy more closely' was denied to German commanders.

In Berlin, SKL repeatedly requested that major surface forces operate in conjunction with U-boats, though it was soon found to be impractical. Originally, fleet-minded officers in SKL viewed U-boats more as a scouting extension to heavily armed warships than a self-contained assault weapon; a position that Karl Dönitz long railed against. Original doctrine indicated that the perfect alignment between air, surface and underwater craft would allow the Luftwaffe to reconnoitre and locate an enemy convoy, major warships to engage the escorts (expected to be destroyers and thus outranged) with main batteries and merchant ships with secondary batteries. Once the escorts were destroyed, all guns would concentrate on destroying merchant ships while U-boats followed and destroyed any ships scattered from the convoy body. In actuality, Luftwaffe reconnaissance was infrequent, and often haphazard and unreliable. Kriegsmarine raiders were forbidden to engage any opposition naval forces of a similar or greater strength and therefore, in the few cases of cooperation between U-boats and surface forces, U-boats were tasked with attempting to disable major enemy escort units so the raiders could engage the convoy. This never came to pass.

The method by which merchant ships were to be attacked was also clearly elaborated on by SKL, an example of their instructions found in an order issued on 22 April 1941 to *Bismarck* and *Prinz Eugen* officers before their Atlantic sortie:

When a weakly escorted convoy is attacked, the convoy commander will certainly disperse his charges. In this case, the first objective must be to disable the largest possible number of steamers by gunfire. (They can be sunk later.) For this, all batteries are to open fire with the exact firing directions and at the lowest possible range appropriate to the calibre. (Main and secondary batteries with nose-fused and base-fused projectiles, heavy flak with nose-fused.) Steamers that have been disabled by gunfire are not to be sunk until not a single steamer is still moving within sight of the ship concerned.

To conserve ammunition, the heavy flak is to be nose-fused and used in the following manner: close within 300–500 meters of the ship, then have the best gunners fire individual shots into the waterline. Fire only when the ship is on the up-roll. Shoot holes in all the steamer's compartments (the largest room is the engine room). With 3.7-centimetre ammunition, shoot holes in the upper part of the steamer, so that during the flooding of the rooms, air can escape upwards.

Prinz Eugen will also use her torpedoes in an attack on a convoy. Against a strongly defended convoy, there will be only a short time, if any, available for the cruiser's attack. This must be exploited as fully as possible. In this case especially, everything will depend on speedy action. The steamers are therefore to be sunk primarily with torpedoes.

The work of destruction may not be delayed by rescue operations.

INTELLIGENCE

Kriegsmarine intelligence was far more effective in some areas than many people are aware. The distribution of Britain's warships was already known to the Kriegsmarine at the outbreak of war thanks to the cryptanalysis department of SKL's naval intelligence unit, located in 72–76 Tirpitzufer in Berlin. Known as the *Beobachtungsdienst*, shortened to B-Dienst, the department had come into its own in 1935 when one of its most gifted operatives, cryptanalyst Wilhelm Tranow, had broken the Royal Navy's most widely used five-digit Naval Administrative Code. Franco's permission to establish listening stations in Spain following the civil war added to the quantity of transmissions Tranow could work with and this cypher, used to communicate between Royal Navy and merchant shipping, was comprehensively penetrated until 1943. French cyphers had posed no such problem and had been compromised quickly.

B-Dienst personnel had numbered only 30 in 1937, but within two years had reached 500 and continued to grow. Initially it was part of an independent department within OKM, headed by *Kapitän zur See* Theodor Arps and known as the Naval Intelligence Service (*Marinenachrichtendienst*). On 1 October 1937 it was incorporated within 3./SKL, *Kapitän zur See* Heinz Bonatz appointed the head of the B-Dienst subsection, which successfully resisted all attempts by the Wehrmacht's Intelligence Service – the Abwehr – to integrate all signals intelligence beneath its singular control. Each major surface ship carried a small number of B-Dienst personnel aboard; cypher and decoding specialists who could keep the ship's operations officers up to date with the latest intercepted information.

The Kriegsmarine used Enigma machines to code and decode messages, the *Heimische* net ('Home', known as 'Dolphin ', to codebreakers at Bletchley Park) was used in home waters, which included the Atlantic. It was broken by

Bletchley Park from 1 August 1941. By that stage, Fleet operations had changed to use the *Neptun* (known to the British as 'Barracuda') from May 1941; a code which was never broken. However, the penetration of other Enigma nets – including that of the Luftwaffe – provided a certain amount of intelligence to the British on major ship movements.

Once at sea, Atlantic raiders transmitted wireless messages sparingly lest they provide direction finding information for the enemy. Commanders had been issued general instructions on the conduct of their mission and a list of operational areas of varying importance. Once in action within the Atlantic, tracking of the ships by MGK West was largely done through intercepted Allied reports and educated guesswork. Ultimately, the success of Allied codebreaking, known as ULTRA, played a small role in countering Atlantic raider operations, but would doom the tanker supply network after the surface ships had withdrawn and the tankers diverted solely to U-boat support.

LOGISTICS AND FACILITIES
Supply Ships

Although there remained some confusion over the actual purpose of the German fleet once war loomed, with a lack of foreign bases, the concept of mobile support for major surface units on Atlantic forays had been established. Each heavy warship was to have its own supply ship that would accompany it into the general area of planned action, combining the roles of tanker, repair ship, ammunition ship and dry cargo ship. Between the warship and supply vessel, six months of consumable supplies could be carried, alongside a large stock of ammunition and fuel. Refuelling was achieved by using the line astern method, rather than the more time efficient but difficult line abreast refuelling style used by the US Navy.

This concept was first tested by the 5,978 GRT tanker MV *Hansa* (its name changed to *Samland* in 1937) after being chartered by the Reichsmarine in 1930 and accompanying the light cruisers *Emden*, *Köln* and *Karlsruhe* on their long-distance training cruises over the following three years. In September 1938, MV *Hansa* acted as supply ship to the *Panzerschiff Deutschland* which took station in the mid-Atlantic after rising tensions with France and the United Kingdom during the Sudeten crisis led to preparations for war. Positioned to be able to attack shipping lanes leading to Europe from South America and South Africa, *Deutschland* first replenished from the tanker *August Schultze* (later renamed *Amerland*) in the Spanish port Vigo. While departing the port, *Deutschland* also made the first operational use of its *Seetakt* radar to slip past shadowing Royal Navy ships in dense fog.

The signing of the Munich Agreement resolved international tensions and *Deutschland* finished its patrol in training manoeuvres with two U-boats, U27 and U30, in which it was discovered impractical to direct U-boats from a surface ship. The successful support of the *Panzerschiff* by *Hansa* led to the full-scale adoption of the concept for all major surface units.

High naval fuel demand presented some problems for the Kriegsmarine, particularly after some 300,000 tons of diesel oil from its strategic reserve was ordered handed over to the army before the western offensive of May 1940 and a further 30,000 tons to German agricultural use. To bolster the prewar import of oil, five naval tankers were constructed; combined oiler and supply ships known as *Trossschiff* which began entering service in 1938. The first of these, 10,816 GRT MT *Dithmarschen*, after which the class was named, was capable of a maximum speed of 23 knots and possessed a range of 12,500nm at 15 knots. It also boasted defensive weaponry consisting of three 150mm/L48 guns (the same as carried on Type 1936A (Mob) destroyers), two 3.7cm and four 2cm anti-aircraft guns, and eight machine guns.

A merchant tanker sinks under fire. The foreground battery is an electrically stabilized twin 10.5cm SK C/33 flak mount. This photograph is frequently misidentified as originating aboard the *Bismarck*, obviously incorrect as *Bismarck* sank no commercial shipping. (Hulton Archive/Getty Images)

A fairly typical converted trawler *Vorpostenboot* photographed in the Bay of Biscay. Workhorses of the Kriegsmarine security flotillas, these hardy vessels provided escort for major ships entering and leaving port, thereby adding their anti-aircraft and anti-submarine capabilities to the procession. (AC)

By the outbreak of war, merchant ships suitable for conversion to supply ships and all available tankers were requisitioned; a move anticipated as far back as 1931 when the directors of Germany's major steamship companies had been approached by the Reichsmarine to compile lists of such suitable ships and their operational characteristics. By June 1940 much extra supply tonnage was acquired from conquered territories and the Kriegsmarine soon possessed a significant supply ship fleet by which Atlantic raiders, U-boats and auxiliary cruisers could be kept at sea. In July 1940, the office of Chief of Supply Ships was established in La Baule, near St Nazaire, under the command of *Fregattenkapitän* Alfred Stiller, his three main bases of operation for the supply ships being Nantes, St Nazaire and Bordeaux.

In action, supply ships were under orders to report to MGK West details of any warships or convoys sighted. In the event of the supply ship coming under attack, the ship's position and the strength of any enemy forces were to be immediately transmitted to MGK West which would in turn communicate such information to any German forces within the vicinity.

The secretive *Etappendienst* played a frequently misunderstood role in supporting Kriegsmarine Atlantic raiders. This service had originated before the previous war and was composed of German nationals or pro-German foreigners that were employed by German steamship lines, oil companies or similar firms engaged in business in foreign countries. By the time of World War II, the Abwehr had secretly re-established this network of operatives, though their remit was limited to countries with which Germany was not in conflict, lest their essential activities in supplying ships at sea be disrupted by intelligence work. Among the myriad tasks undertaken by this secretive organization – including the extremely successful covert resupply of U-boats within Spanish harbours – was that a small number of supply ships and tankers were refuelled and despatched at various times from South America to support surface raiders and auxiliary cruisers; the *Etappendienst* area chief, *Kapitän zur See* Dietrich Niebuhr, was also the naval attaché in Buenos Aires (expelled by the Argentinians for espionage in 1943).

The French Bases

The acquisition of French Atlantic bases in June 1940 was exactly what the Kriegsmarine needed to strengthen its assault upon Allied Atlantic merchant shipping. Whereas before the fall of France, German vessels headed to the Atlantic had been forced to journey 450nm through the North Sea and around the north of the United Kingdom, they were now directly on the Atlantic fringe. U-boat flotillas began the task of moving their administrative stations to three ports: Brest, Lorient and St Nazaire, with Italian submarines soon moving to Bordeaux and La Rochelle (La Pallice). The latter would also host German U-boats from late 1941 onwards.

Preceding the U-boats' relocation, smaller vessels of the security flotillas arrived on the French Atlantic coast as MGK West oversaw the establishment of the necessary logistical framework under which each port would operate. Immediately upon the French surrender, stocks of captured weapons, fuel, supplies and ships were examined by German officers despatched immediately to hasten the ports' levels of readiness. Clear channels were swept through minefields laid by both the Allies and Luftwaffe, and anti-aircraft units were swiftly installed at critical points as coastal artillery positions began construction.

The supply of skilled dockyard workers was a recurring difficulty, somewhat assuaged by the labour pool found in newly conquered territories. Engineers, technicians and dockyard workers of the occupied countries worked within shipyards and ports which both maintained naval vessels and converted new ones. In France, some 2,000 men worked for the Kriegsmarine in this capacity, authorized by the Vichy government at the beginning of August 1940, although workers in Brest and Lorient had already started on the conversion of trawlers to *Vorpostenboote*. It was not until March 1944 that Frenchmen and other European volunteers could enlist for service within the ranks of the Kriegsmarine itself.

The mine clearance vessel *Sperrbrecher 19 Rostock* leading *Scharnhorst* towards Brest harbour in 1941. *Rostock* was based on the Atlantic coast from May 1941, its minesweeping capabilities essential as RAF bombing raids became frequently interspersed with minelaying off the occupied Atlantic ports. This photograph perfectly illustrates the *Sperrbrecher*'s task of, if all other minesweeping systems fail, sailing into enemy mines and detonating them instead of damage being inflicted on *Scharnhorst*. (AC)

The *Führer der Minensuchboote* Friedrich Ruge had personally travelled aboard the *Räumboot R27* to bays flanking Brest to oversee the selection of French vessels suitable for requisitioning by the Germans as minesweepers. His primary concern was the immediate establishment of security forces for permanent stationing in the French ports. An officer and 100 men were ordered to Brest from the minesweeping personnel reserve in Cuxhaven, while the 3. R-Flotilla was moved from Denmark to France immediately. Newly established 4. R-Flotilla began Channel operations and the 2. R-Flotilla, already having swept the entrance to major harbours from Le Havre to Lorient, was then engaged on escort for occupation troops and prisoners to and from Ouessant before being posted to Boulogne and St Nazaire. Meanwhile, dozens of captured vessels were swiftly converted to military use and added to the inventories of all German harbour defence units. For major surface vessels, two of the captured Atlantic bases provided the necessary amenities: Brest and St Nazaire (Lorient was considered capable of only servicing a single light cruiser at any given time).

Brest had long been an established French military port and its capture provided the Germans with a bounty of facilities. Within the military harbour at Laninon, French graving docks Nos 8 and 9 could accommodate major surface vessels, measuring 250m by 36m apiece. A short distance along the Penfeld River, before the existing Arsenal buildings and Rue du Pontaniou, were two further graving docks: No. 2 measuring 178m by 27m, and Pontaniou No. 3 at 178m by 33m; perfect for the maintenance of security vessels such as minesweepers and patrol boats. In the Commercial Dock to the east of the Penfeld entrance lay one further dry dock 225m in length, named *Bassin Redoub Commerce No. 1*. In St Nazaire, the long-established shipbuilding yard that contained the 350m x 50m Louis Joubert Lock and Graving Dock (frequently called the 'Normandie Dock'), provided the only such facility in France capable of taking Germany's largest battleships.

However, on 3 December 1941, in after-dinner conversation with *Admiral* Otto Schultze (*Kommandierender Admiral Frankreich*), François Darlan (*Amiral de la flotte* and Deputy Prime Minister of Vichy France) urged the Kriegsmarine never to take a 35,000-ton warship into the St Nazaire dock as it would amount to an almost 'certain loss of this ship for at least a year' due to the difficulties presented by water depth and local conditions that prohibited moving such a fully loaded vessel in and out of the dock.

A great deal of effort was expended in defences for the major French harbours. Though part of the expansive Atlantic Wall, they were accorded extra defensive measures due to the importance attached to the naval infrastructure being developed, particularly at Brest. While Lorient would become the centre of

RENDEZVOUS OFF BREST HARBOUR

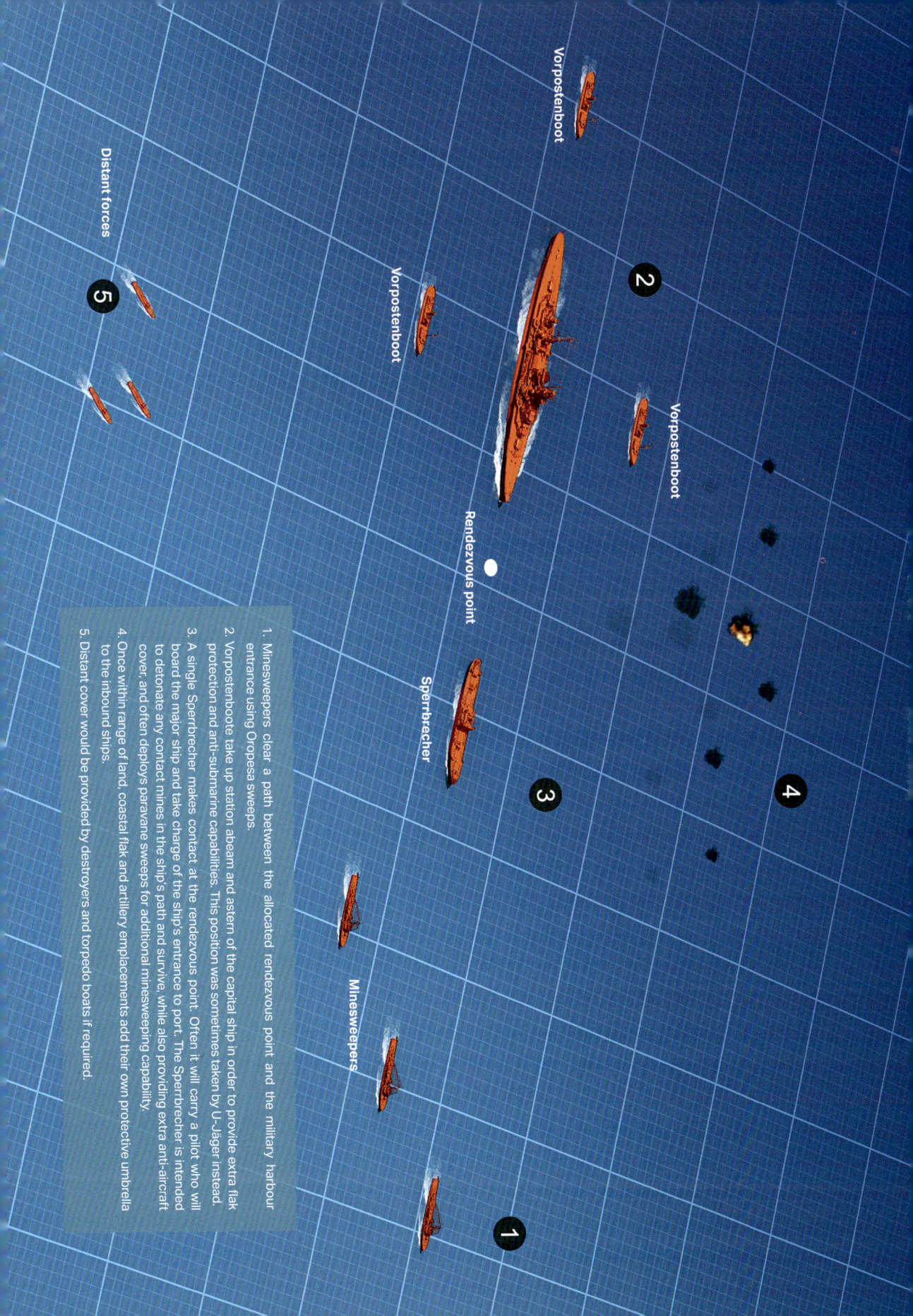

Vorpostenboot

Vorpostenboot

Distant forces

Vorpostenboot

Rendezvous point

Sperrbrecher

Minesweepers

1. Minesweepers clear a path between the allocated rendezvous point and the military harbour entrance using Oropesa sweeps.

2. Vorpostenboote take up station abeam and astern of the capital ship in order to provide extra flak protection and anti-submarine capabilities. This position was sometimes taken by U-Jäger instead.

3. A single Sperrbrecher makes contact at the rendezvous point. Often it will carry a pilot who will board the major ship and take charge of the ship's entrance to port. The Sperrbrecher is intended to detonate any contact mines in the ship's path and survive, while also providing extra anti-aircraft cover, and often deploys paravane sweeps for additional minesweeping capability.

4. Once within range of land, coastal flak and artillery emplacements add their own protective umbrella to the inbound ships.

5. Distant cover would be provided by destroyers and torpedo boats if required.

gravity for U-boat maintenance and repair, Brest was designated the primary port for surface ships, despite the St Nazaire dry dock being the only one capable of handling ships of the *Bismarck*'s size.

According to standing regulations, Brest's anti-aircraft defence lay in the hands of the Luftwaffe and, as such, the commander of the Luftwaffe's *Flak Regiment* 100, *Oberstleutnant* Franz Engel, was in overall control, with naval flak at his disposal. In

Gneisenau in Brest dry dock. The port pair of spherical armoured 'Wobble Pot' flak rangefinders stand out in this image, as does the 'mattress' aerial for the *Seetakt* radar attached to the uppermost rangefinder. (AC)

and around Brest itself, *Korvettenkapitän* Dr Max Grotewahl's *Marine Flak Abteilung* 803 was responsible for the lion's share of anti-aircraft defence, though the Luftwaffe's 4./Res. *Flak Abteilung* 193 had already situated its guns in the commercial port and the arsenal on the Penfeld River. Luftwaffe installations were later replaced in the years between 1942 and 1944 as the Kriegsmarine added additional batteries to defend Brest, despite the absence of major surface vessels. By that stage, the Atlantic had become the domain of the U-boats, and Brest remained a high-target priority due to the presence of two U-boat flotillas and several supporting flotillas of small surface craft that would become the targets of dedicated RAF and Royal Navy operations in 1943/44. A small number of Italian artillerymen were also present in the Brest area, manning an Italian artillery emplacement near the *Goulet de Brest*.

The anti-aircraft batteries that ringed what would become, in 1944, 'Festung Brest' (Fortress Brest) would come to be deployed in an arc approximately 4km from the city centre. Eventually numbering five different *Flak Abteilung*, they were designated *Marine Flak Regiment 24* in December 1941, changed to *III. Marine Flak Brigade* on 1 April 1943. By that stage there were 30 separate anti-aircraft and searchlight batteries.

Brest was also extremely well covered by coastal artillery batteries that again developed as the war years passed. Though a severe deterrent to surface attack – as well as each coastal battery installation having its own flak guns – there were limited forays towards Brest by Allied destroyers and MTBs in the years after the departure of the capital ships. Army units would also begin to establish coastal artillery positions, but very few saw any action except facing inland against the American advance in 1944. The biggest batter, 'Graf Spee,' situated near Le Conquet, is the only one of these to offer a significant engagement to a major warship when it engaged in an inconclusive duel with battleship HMS *Warspite* in August 1944.

COMBAT AND ANALYSIS

THE FLEET IN COMBAT
1939

With the declaration of war by Britain and France on 3 September, Raeder faced his greatest fear; combat of an incomplete Kriegsmarine against the Royal Navy. The doctrine applied to major surface operations had remained somewhat makeshift as the drift to war accelerated and German fortunes were not aided by Hitler's sudden vacillation regarding the opening of attacks on British Atlantic merchant shipping. Both *Deutschland* and *Admiral Graf Spee* were on station within their predetermined holding areas and yet over three weeks passed before clarification of their tasks arrived from SKL. This delay was especially unfortunate as both *Panzerschiff* commanders later regretted their inability to intercept solo sailing merchant vessels that were periodically seen before convoy formation took firm hold. However, Hitler believed that with

A view of the entrance to the Penfeld River, Brest, photographed shortly after its capture. The port was designated by the Kriegsmarine as the primary location for supporting surface raiding operations. The Penfeld housed an established French armoury while the military harbour contained two dry docks capable of taking all but the largest German battleships. (AC)

Wilhelm Meisel, commander of the *Admiral Hipper* during its Atlantic missions, pictured here with the rank of *Admiral* to which he was promoted on 1 April 1944. At that point he was the Chief of SKL. (AC)

the collapse of Poland, peace overtures made towards Great Britain could yet halt all-out war. Despite U-boats having gone into limited action from 3 September – including the unexpected and mistaken sinking of British liner SS *Athenia* by *U30* – severe restrictions had been applied to both Kriegsmarine and Luftwaffe offensive operations against France and Great Britain.

During late September 1939, SKL planned the equipping of six auxiliary cruisers, heavily armed and able to traverse the oceans with an endurance of 12 months from use of their own onboard supplies, in operational areas expected to include the South Atlantic, Indian and Pacific Oceans; beyond that, resupply from the *Etappendienst* would be necessary. Each ship would adopt disguise as a powerful method of operation and, though expected to be ready by November, the first – *HSK 2 'Atlantis'* – did not sail until 31 March 1940 after the most severe winter weather in recent history caused unexpected delays. MGK West was responsible for the sailing of these disguised auxiliary cruisers into the North Sea until they reached 60°N in the North Atlantic, or 40°E into the Arctic. After that, they were under SKL's direct command. Their operations will not feature in this text as they roamed far beyond the Atlantic Ocean.

On 23 September SKL *Konteradmiral* Otto Schniewind held a conference with Hitler at the latter's temporary headquarters in the Grand Hotel at Zoppot, near Danzig. Schniewind argued that the two *Panzerschiffe* already at sea *must* go into action by the beginning of October lest they face not only a supply shortage, having already consumed over a quarter of their fuel, but also a severely detrimental effect on crew morale. *Deutschland* had replenished from its supporting tanker *Westerwald* on 30 August but had still expended valuable supplies while moving within its waiting area south of Greenland. Likewise, *Admiral Graf Spee* had made its first rendezvous with *Altmark* in the mid-Atlantic south-west of the Canary Islands on 1 September to also refuel before continuing south towards Brazil and its waiting area 900nm east of Bahia. *Kapitän zur See* Hans Langsdorff's ship had already lost its first casualty on 26 August when Petty Officer Matzger lost his footing in heavy seas and was swept overboard by a wave as he headed a small working party that was attempting to secure the ship's bow anchor chains. Two hours of searching failed to locate the missing man. Langsdorff, a veteran of World War I, hailed from the island of Rügen and ironically had been a neighbour to Graf Maximilian von Spee, who achieved fame as an admiral in the 1914 Battle of the Falklands. Aboard *Deutschland*, *Kapitän zur See* Paul Wenneker was also a veteran of the previous war, after which he continued to serve in the Reichsmarine and was Germany's naval attaché to Tokyo between 1933 and 1937.

With the lines now more firmly drawn between Germany and Western Allies, Hitler relented and allowed operations to begin, and three days later both *Admiral Graf Spee* and *Deutschland* were ordered to leave their waiting areas – though SKL was unaware of their exact locations but acting on presumption – and commence hostilities against enemy merchant shipping.

German naval intelligence placed British battlecruisers within home waters or the North Sea, and so both *Panzerschiffe* were instructed to begin short aggressive thrusts into their operational areas; *Deutschland* in the North Atlantic and *Graf Spee* in the South. It was expected that the presence of the pocket battleships would soon become known and superior enemy forces be sent to find them. Both German ship commanders were under orders to shift their operational area frequently and disappear into the expanse of the ocean, lest the enemy be able to locate and surround them, undoubtedly gaining a great deal of prestige if they succeeded in destroying the German pocket battleships.

The *Graf Spee* and *Altmark* had been travelling in loose company with further refuelling carried out, and Langsdorff lightened his ship's load by transferring or jettisoning superfluous material. British attention was evaded through reconnaissance by *Graf Spee*'s Ar. 196 floatplane as Langsdorff kept his ship's carpenters busy disguising *Graf Spee*. The ship was sometimes made to resemble British or French warships by the addition of a fake 'B' turret and false funnel, and by painting the superstructure to appear to be a tripod mast. False bow waves were painted on the hull to mislead observers as to the ship's size, distance and speed. Fuel was conserved by engines being periodically shut down, allowing the ship to drift for up to six hours at a time. The two ships finally parted company on 27 September, with future rendezvous plans already logged.

On 30 September the *Spee*'s Arado aircraft located solitary freighter SS *Clement* and passed low over the bow as *Graf Spee* approached. When the pocket battleship was sighted, *Clement* increased speed. Warned not to transmit, the Arado dived to repeatedly strafe after radio signals of 'RRR' ('Am being attacked by raider') were detected. The machine-gun fire injured the Chief Officer until Captain Frederick Harris ordered radio silence and jettisoned all secret material. *Clement* came to a halt and a German boarding party arrived to confirm the presence of contraband in accordance with international prize law. Harris and Chief Engineer Walter Bryant were taken back aboard *Graf Spee* while the remaining 47 crew abandoned ship in four lifeboats. Once clear, scuttling charges were detonated, though they frustratingly failed to sink *Clement*. Two torpedoes both malfunctioned and missed, and

Admiral Hipper in the Laninon 8 dry dock at Brest, January 1941. In the background the mole protecting the military harbour is visible as are several *Sperrbrecher*, acting as moored flak ships. (Carlo Maggio / Alamy Stock Photo)

RAIDER OPERATIONAL AREAS

SHIPS SUNK, CAPTURED OR HEAVILY DAMAGED BY ATLANTIC RAIDERS

1939

1	30 September SS *Clement* 5,050 GRT (*Admiral Graf Spee*)
2	5 October SS *Newton Beech* 4,615 GRT, captured, later sunk on 8 October (*Admiral Graf Spee*)
3	5 October SS *Stonegate* 5,044 GRT (*Deutschland*)
4	7 October SS *Ashlea* 4,222 GRT (*Admiral Graf Spee*)
5	9 October SS *City of Flint*, captured but later lost and returned to USA (*Deutschland*)
6	10 October SS *Huntsman* 8,196 GRT captured, later sunk on 17 October (*Admiral Graf Spee*)
7	14 October SS *Lorent W. Hansen* 1,918 GRT (*Deutschland*)
8	22 October SS *Trevanion*, 5,299 GRT (*Admiral Graf Spee*)
9	15 November MV *Africa Shell* 706 GRT (*Admiral Graf Spee*)
10	2 December SS *Doric Star* 6,347 GRT (*Admiral Graf Spee*)
11	3 December SS *Tairoa* 7,983 GRT (*Admiral Graf Spee*)
12	7 December SS *Streonshalh* 3,895 GRT (*Admiral Graf Spee*)

1940

13	5 November SS *Mopan* 5,389 GRT (*Admiral Scheer*)
14	5 November HMS *Jervis Bay* AMC (*Admiral Scheer*) (Convoy HX84)
15	5 November SS *Beaverford* 10,042 GRT (*Admiral Scheer*) (Convoy HX84)
16	5 November MV *Fresno City* 4,955 GRT (*Admiral Scheer*) (Convoy HX84)
17	5 November SS *Kenbane Head* 5,225 GRT (*Admiral Scheer*) (Convoy HX84)
18	5 November SS *Maidan* 7,908 GRT (*Admiral Scheer*) (Convoy HX84)
19	5 November MV *San Demetrio*, damaged but reached the Clyde 16 November (*Admiral Scheer*) (Convoy HX84)
20	5 November SS *Trewellard* 5,201 GRT (*Admiral Scheer*) (Convoy HX84)
21	24 November MV *Port Hobart* 7,448 GRT (*Admiral Scheer*)
22	1 December SS *Tribesman* 6,242 GRT (*Admiral Scheer*)
23	18 December SS *Duquesa* 8,651 GRT captured, later sunk on 18 February (*Admiral Scheer*)
24	25 December SS *Jumna* 6,078 GRT (*Admiral Hipper*)

1941

25	18 January MT *Sandefjord* 8,038 GRT captured, entered Gironde 27 February (*Admiral Scheer*)
26	20 January SS *Barnveldt* 5,554 GRT captured, sunk next day (*Admiral Scheer*)
27	20 January SS *Stanpark* 5,103 GRT (*Admiral Scheer*)
28	11 February SS *Iceland* 1,225 GRT (*Admiral Hipper*)
29	12 February SS *Shrewsbury* 4,542 GRT (*Admiral Hipper*) (Convoy SLS64)
30	12 February SS *Warlaby* 4,876 GRT (*Admiral Hipper*) (Convoy SLS64)
31	12 February SS *Derrynane* 4,896 GRT (*Admiral Hipper*) (Convoy SLS64)
32	12 February SS *Westbury* 4,712 GRT (*Admiral Hipper*) (Convoy SLS64)
33	12 February SS *Perseus* 5,178 GRT (*Admiral Hipper*) (Convoy SLS64)
34	12 February MV *Borgestad* 3,924 GRT (*Admiral Hipper*) (Convoy SLS64)
35	12 February SS *Oswestry Grange* 4,684 GRT (*Admiral Hipper*) (Convoy SLS64)
36	20 February SS *British Advocate* 6,994 GRT captured, entered Bordeaux 29 April (*Admiral Scheer*)
37	20 February SS *Grigorius C. II* 2,546 GRT (*Admiral Scheer*)
38	21 February SS *Canadian Cruiser* 7,178 GRT (*Admiral Scheer*)
39	22 February SS *Rantaupandjang* 2,542 GRT (*Admiral Scheer*)
40	22 February SS *A. D. Huff* 6,219 GRT (*Gneisenau*)
41	22 February SS *Trelawny* 4,689 GRT (*Gneisenau*)
42	22 February SS *Harlesden* 5,483 GRT (*Gneisenau*)
43	22 February SS *Kantara* 3,237 GRT (*Gneisenau*)
44	22 February SS *Lustrous* 6,156 GRT (*Scharnhorst*)
45	9 March SS *Marathon* 8,010 GRT (*Scharnhorst*)
46	15 March MV *Athelfoam* 6,554 GRT (*Scharnhorst*)
47	15 March MT *Bianca* 5,688 GRT captured but sunk five days later (*Gneisenau*)
48	15 March MT *Polykarp* 6,405 GRT captured and reached Gironde on 24 March (*Scharnhorst*)
49	15 March MV *British Strength* 7,139 GRT (*Scharnhorst*)
50	15 March SS *Myson* 4,564 GRT (*Gneisenau*)
51	15 March SS *Rio Dorado* 4,507 GRT (*Gneisenau*)
52	15 March SS *Royal Crown* 4,364 GRT (*Gneisenau*)
53	15 March MV *San Casimiro* 8,046 GRT captured and later sunk on 20 March (*Gneisenau*)
54	15 March MV *Simnia* 6,197 GRT (*Gneisenau*)
55	16 March MV *Chilean Reefer* 1,831 GRT (*Gneisenau*)
56	16 March SS *Demeterton* 5,251 GRT (*Scharnhorst*)
57	16 March SS *Empire Industry* 3,721 GRT (*Gneisenau*)
58	16 March SS *Granli* 1,577 GRT (*Gneisenau*)
59	16 March SS *Mangkai* 8,135 GRT (*Scharnhorst*)
60	16 March SS *Sardinian Prince* 3,491 GRT (*Scharnhorst*)
61	16 March MV *Silverfir* 4,347 GRT (*Scharnhorst*)

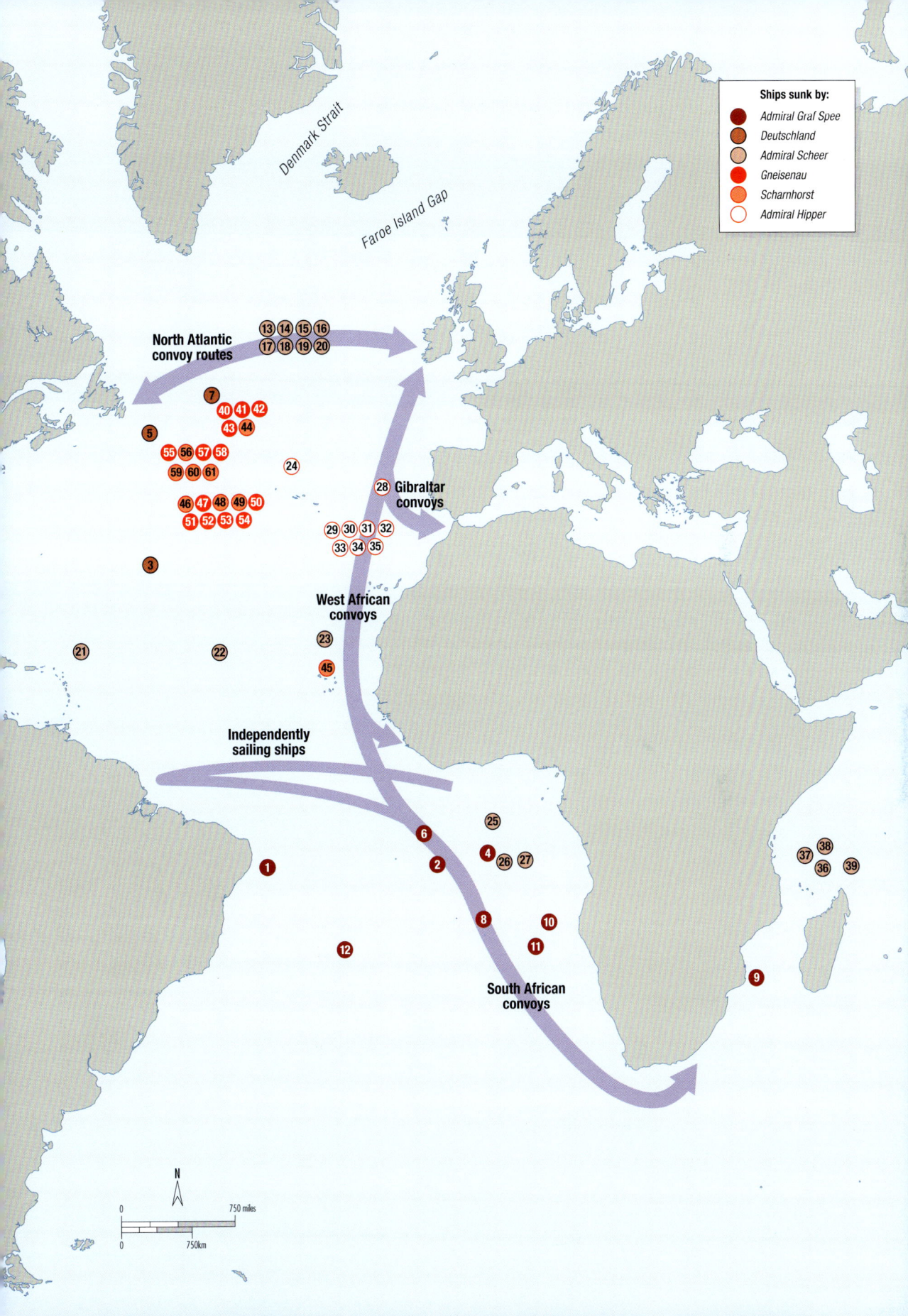

Ships sunk by:
- Admiral Graf Spee
- Deutschland
- Admiral Scheer
- Gneisenau
- Scharnhorst
- Admiral Hipper

Denmark Strait

Faroe Island Gap

North Atlantic convoy routes

Gibraltar convoys

West African convoys

Independently sailing ships

South African convoys

N

0   750 miles

0   750km

Langsdorff ordered the secondary batteries to open fire at only 300m range. Twenty-five rounds still failed to sink the ship and 11 rounds from the main guns finally sent the ship to the bottom; *Clement* was the first ship of the war to be sunk by a surface raider. Meanwhile, Langsdorff had despatched a distress signal on behalf of the *Clement's* crew to the Brazilian naval station in Pernambuco, and they were subsequently rescued by a steamer and landed in Brazil. Later that evening, *Graf Spee* intercepted and stopped Greek tramp steamer SS *Papalemos*. Travelling in company and observing radio silence until a significant distance had been covered, Langsdorff released his two captives to the Greeks.

As news of the presence of a German surface raider in the South Atlantic broke in Whitehall – misidentified as the *Admiral Scheer* due to misinformation planted with the *Clement's* crew – the British and French navies swiftly formed eight hunting groups. While merchant sailings from Rio de Janeiro and Santos were suspended for four days, British aircraft carriers HMS *Hermes*, *Eagle* and *Ark Royal*, the French aircraft carrier *Béarn*, British battlecruiser *Renown*, and French battleships *Dunkerque* and *Strasbourg*, were all committed along with 15 cruisers. To form these groups, the Royal Navy had been forced to siphon strength from its Home Fleet; exactly the kind of dispersal of strength that Raeder had hoped to accomplish. Furthermore, three British battleships and two cruisers had been posted to escort North Atlantic convoys and another battleship and carrier moved from the Mediterranean Sea to the Indian Ocean.

Of those groups tasked with scouring the South Atlantic, Force G, commanded by Commodore Henry Harwood, was assigned to the east coast of South America. Harwood controlled cruisers HMS *Cumberland* – which had already unknowingly passed by *Graf Spee* without a sighting – and *Exeter*. They were soon reinforced by light cruisers HMS *Ajax* and *Achilles* after which Harwood detached *Cumberland* to the Falkland Islands while the remainder patrolled the approaches to the River Plate.

RAF No. 22 Squadron Beauforts having their torpedoes readied for operations, 1941. (De Luan/ Alamy Stock Photo)

Far to the east of the location of its previous victim, *Graf Spee* encountered steamer SS *Newton Beech*, Langsdorff approaching while flying the French flag, only struck and replaced by the Kriegsmarine ensign at a range of 1,800m. Despite orders not to transmit, the 'RRR' signal was once again sent along with the ship's location before a German prize crew boarded, recovering a quantity of papers before they could be thrown overboard. The decision was made not to sink the steamer and 2.5 tons of cargo were eventually taken aboard *Graf Spee*, which now travelled in loose formation with *Altmark* and the captured *Newton Beech*.

Meanwhile, 400nm east of Bermuda, on that same day, *Deutschland* had struck its first blow by sinking 5,044 GRT SS *Stonegate*. On passage from Antofagaste to Alexandria with a cargo of nitrate, the British steamer transmitted its 'RRR' signal before warning shots from *Deutschland* made the crew abandon ship. Given 15 minutes to get clear, they were taken aboard the raider as *Stonegate* was destroyed with gunfire.

The dislocation caused by the appearance of the two raiders had almost surpassed expectations and before the month's end between them they had sunk seven ships and captured two others. Furthermore, raider hysteria began to infect the region; an American steamer reported sighting the *Admiral Scheer* 60 miles east of Natal while several German 'warcraft' were reported by observers off Puerta Deseardo in Patagonia. *Deutschland* would ultimately only sink two ships during its voyage and seize the American SS *City of Flint* on 9 October, the ship travelling from New York with a cargo of tractors, grain and fruit for Britain. Wenneker, declaring the cargo contraband, took the ship and put a prize crew aboard to sail to Kiel under the German flag. This began a confused odyssey which saw the steamer arrive in Norway after suffering weather damage, be refused permission to anchor and move to Murmansk where it was able to moor for repairs before heading to Norway once again. This time, the steamer was boarded by a Norwegian naval party and restored to American control, the *Deutschland*'s prize crew interned and *City of Flint* unloaded its cargo in Bergen, Norway, before returning to New York. Interestingly, the British newspaper *Daily Herald* reported the *City of Flint* as having been seized by light cruiser *Emden*.

After barely a month in action, Hitler had already expressed a desire to recall *Deutschland* as soon as possible so that it could be renamed lest the ship be caught by the Royal Navy and sunk. Such an omen, he felt, would severely affect German morale. Although Raeder initially recommended that *Deutschland* stay on station, by 28 October SKL was also sensing that the time was right to perhaps recall both ships.

Schniewind proffered the point of view that with Royal Navy pressure increasing on the two raiders it would perhaps be wise for both ships to return to home waters in November. The withdrawal of the heavy British forces from the North Sea and their concentration in the Atlantic for the safeguarding of convoy traffic as well as the pursuit of the pocket battleships no longer promised substantial prospects of success in the Atlantic. Their primary task – damage of enemy merchant traffic by direct attack – was no longer considered profitable. On the other hand, the additional objectives of affecting merchant traffic volume and the tying-down of strong enemy forces with its resultant increased wear and tear, had already been fully achieved.

Now, Schniewind felt, prudence dictated that the preservation of both *Panzerschiffe* and their restoration to full operational readiness for future opportunities must take precedence. Any loss of German prestige and resultant rise in enemy stature must be avoided at all costs. The Royal Navy was still

Kapitän zur See Hans Langsdorff and some of his crew. After being misled by the Royal Navy as to their strength off Montevideo, rather than sacrifice his men in what he regarded to be a futile battle he chose to scuttle *Graf Spee*, later committing suicide as he symbolically went down with his ship. (Süeddeutsche Zeitung Photo/Alamy Foto Stock)

reeling from the sinking of HMS *Royal Oak* within the protected anchorage of Scapa Flow by *U47* and the successful return of the raiders would only add to British misery. Additionally, there was vague expectation that Italy, and perhaps Spain, would enter the war on the Axis side which would have far-reaching consequences on the disposition of British and French naval and air forces. They would be compelled to reinforce the Mediterranean, presenting more favourable opportunities for surface raiders within the Atlantic once again: 'The objective must therefore be to have the *Panzerschiffe* available once more in full operational readiness at that time – which Naval Staff expects to be in spring 1940 – in the Atlantic where their operations can then be most effectively supported by the appearance of the auxiliary cruisers.'[9]

Both *Panzerschiffe* required major engine overhauls not later than January 1940 and with longer November nights and potentially bad weather looming, the resultant poor visibility would favour the breakthrough of ships back into the North Sea. Correspondingly, the decision was taken that *Deutschland* would be the first to leave its patrol. Relevant orders were issued and on the night of 8 November *Deutschland* successfully slipped through the Denmark Strait, headed north-east. Within a week, *Deutschland* docked in the Baltic port of Gotenhafen. There the ship was almost immediately officially renamed *Lützow* by Raeder. Supporting tanker *Westerwald* followed, passing through the Great Belt into the Baltic on 22 November. As the first German Atlantic raider to return from its mission, Wenneker was promoted during February to *Konteradmiral* and returned to his position as naval attaché to Japan. The ship's refit was completed during March 1940 and intentions were to despatch *Lützow* on a commerce-raiding operation into the South Atlantic. The ship, however, would never reach the Atlantic again.

By the end of November *Graf Spee* had sunk its sixth ship, the British 706 GRT coastal tanker MS *Africa Shell*. Langsdorff had taken *Graf Spee* into the Indian Ocean to confuse its pursuers, encountering the tanker in the Mozambique Channel. A warning shot across the bow stopped the ship which possessed no wireless and so was unable to transmit the 'RRR' message. After the ship was boarded, the crew were ordered into their lifeboats, apart from Captain Patrick Dove who was taken back to *Graf Spee*. The small tanker was then sunk by two scuttling charges, the crew

9   SKL KTB, 28 October 1939.

reaching Lourenco Marques later that day and reporting their sinking by the '*Admiral Scheer*'.

By this stage, *Graf Spee* required an engine overhaul, with several cracks appearing in the engine housings due to constant vibration. As Langsdorff judged their Indian Ocean foray to hold little promise, *Graf Spee* returned to the South Atlantic to rendezvous with *Altmark*. Two more ships – SS *Doric Star* and SS *Tairou* – were intercepted and sunk, their crews and most other prisoners transferred to *Altmark*.

In Berlin, SKL agreed to *Graf Spee*'s return for an extensive dockyard overhaul during January 1940. Estimated voyage time required Langsdorff to begin return passage at the beginning of December and until then deployment of the ship was left to the captain's discretion. Langsdorff made the fatal decision to head west towards the River Plate, during the evening of 7 December claiming his final victim when *Graf Spee* intercepted and sank British freighter SS *Streonshalh*.

By this stage the ship's aircraft was out of action with severe structural and engine damage, and *Graf Spee* was denied aerial reconnaissance ability. No doubt this did not help the decision to engage what at first was taken to be a British convoy sighted early morning on 13 December. Mastheads sighted were at first thought to be a cruiser and two destroyers escorting merchants, but soon revealed themselves to be Force G: heavy cruiser HMS *Exeter* and light cruisers HMS *Ajax* and *Achilles*. The resultant battle is well documented (See CAM 171: *River Plate 1939*, Osprey Books, 2016) and resulted in severe damage to *Exeter* and *Ajax* but also 37 German crew killed and 60 wounded. Crucially, the *Graf Spee*'s ancillary boiler, which formed a vital link in the water desalination plant and the oil purification plant required to prepare the diesel fuel for the engines, had been destroyed. The galleys had been wrecked and the ship was in no condition for a potential return through North Atlantic winter conditions. Langsdorff subsequently retreated into Montevideo and would later scuttle his ship after being convinced by British intelligence deception that he faced an overwhelming enemy when forced to leave the neutral port. The decision to scuttle or fight had been left to Langsdorff and, rather than sacrifice his men in a battle he believed he could not win, he scuttled in the harbour roadstead on 17 December. Three days later he shot himself after taking full responsibility in a letter to Raeder for the loss of his ship. Hitler was predictably outraged at what he took to be a lack of fighting spirit and refused to see the naval, and indeed humanitarian, justification for Langsdorff's actions.

1940

The new year dawned with U-boats as the sole German force in action within the Atlantic Ocean, their number wholly insufficient for the task of disrupting convoy traffic. On the French Atlantic coast, German destroyers featured little, reaching

Propaganda image of *Admiral Scheer* published as a cigarette card to be included in the NSDAP published book *Adolf Hitler: Photos from the Führer's Life* from 1936. (AC)

an early peak in late 1940 at the western edge of the English Channel. Five destroyers – *Z6 Theodor Reidel*, *Z14 Friedrich Ihn*, *Z10 Hans Lody*, *Z16 Friedrich Eckoldt* and *Z20 Karl Gastner* – arrived in Brest on the morning of 20 September and were the first major German warships to enter the port. Bolstered by the arrival of *Z15 Erich Steinbrinck* and *Z5 Paul Jacobi* three days later they were grouped into two flotillas: 5. and 6. *Zerstörerflottille*. Under the overall command of *Kapitän zur See* Erich Jakob Bey they embarked upon a mine offensive against England, laying a minefield outside of Falmouth harbour which claimed five small British ships totalling 2,037 GRT and minesweeping trawler HMT *Comet*.

British air raids on these ships in Brest produced limited results, though a raid by the Fleet Air Arm's 829 Naval Air Squadron from St Eval on the night of 9 October lightly damaged three of the nuisance destroyers with bomb splinters and strafing. Two destroyer crewmen were killed in the attack and another seven wounded while a single Albacore bomber piloted by the squadron leader, Lieutenant Commander O.S. Stevinson, was shot down by flak and crashed near Porspoder with all three crewmen captured. Further operations by Bey's destroyers resulted in a fierce cannon and torpedo duel against the Royal Navy's Force F of two light cruisers and five destroyers. Despite long-distance artillery salvoes, torpedo spreads and Luftwaffe attack in support of the retreating German destroyers there were no casualties to either side.

The number of Bey's destroyers fluctuated as ships departed for refit in Germany until Bey held only three destroyers. However, even this small unit made its presence felt. In the pouring rain and high seas of 24 November, they attacked what they believed was a convoy near Wolf Rock. Fortunately, the 'convoy' was soon identified as nothing more than fishing trawlers and the Germans disengaged. Within two hours however three merchant ships were sighted and attacked, this time sending the Dutch 2,156 GRT MV *Appolonia* to the bottom. Alerted by the flash of distant gunfire, the Royal Navy's 5th Destroyer Flotilla hunted for the elusive Germans but failed to find them in the driving rain.

Three nights later, the trio of German destroyers sank a barge and tugboat in the same area before being intercepted by British destroyers. At 0630hrs with dawn still two hours away, the battle unfolded quickly, each German ship launching four torpedoes before bolting for Brest, observing standing orders not to directly engage enemy forces of any significant strength. HMS *Javelin* was seriously damaged by gunfire and torpedoes from *Z10* that blew off both the bow and stern, though the ship was safely towed to harbour for repairs. This marked the end of the German destroyers' first deployment in Brest and by January they had departed for Germany, their place taken by the torpedo boats of the 5. and 6. *Torpedobootflottille* with no more destroyers on the French Atlantic coast until March 1943.

In Germany, *Admiral Scheer* had been undergoing a thorough refit and was officially reclassified as a heavy cruiser. Modifications included the fitting of a raked clipper bow, replacement of the heavy command tower with a lighter structure and additional anti-aircraft guns installed along with updated radar equipment. On 27 July *Admiral Scheer* was pronounced ready for service with *Kapitän zur See* Theodore Krancke in command, proceeding to the Baltic for trials until September.

Following his return with *Deutschland* in December 1939, Wenneker had pushed for a combined operation of two pocket battleships operating together to increase the potential damage that could be inflicted upon the enemy. In Berlin, however, SKL reasoned that as the pocket battleships' assignment was not simply action but the achievement of a strong diversionary effect, while close tactical connection of two major ships would force the enemy to appear in greater strength, they would have only *one* area and *one* battlegroup to hunt. The principle remained, at that point, more practical to despatch Atlantic raiders singly.

Thus, it was on 23 October that *Admiral Scheer* departed Gotenhafen to pass through the Kiel Canal and head into the North Sea under torpedo boat escort. Krancke had been briefed to pursue the primary purpose of tying down enemy forces for the relief of the home area, while also inflicting damage on the enemy; his initial instructions to attack the convoy route of ships travelling between Halifax, Nova Scotia and Great Britain. Following that, dependent on enemy reaction, he was presented with a range of potential target areas including the traffic lane of independent shipping traversing from the West Indies to Africa, South Atlantic traffic routes between La Plata and Freetown, or the Cape and Freetown, whaling areas of the Antarctic between December and February, or even the Pacific Ocean. The heavy cruiser would be supported by the tanker *Nordmark*.

Admiral Scheer passed through the Denmark Strait on the last day of October and B-Dienst almost immediately informed Krancke of a large convoy,

Admiral Scheer photographed in Gibraltar during its part in the non-interventionist patrol of Spain during the civil war. (Shawshots/Alamy Stock Photo)

HX84, which had departed Halifax, Nova Scotia, on 27 October. Krancke proceeded to place *Scheer* astride the presumed convoy route, passing up the chance to attack two separately sighted ships for fear of alerting the inbound convoy to his presence. The single Arado Ar196 reconnaissance aircraft had been prevented from flying due to inclement weather but, on 5 November, was successfully launched and observer *Oberleutnant zur See* Ulrich Pietsch subsequently reported eight ships approaching some 90nm away with no discernible escort, though further indistinct vessels were visible in the distance. Krancke's calculations for interception allowed only two hours of full light in which to attack, but he seized the opportunity and ordered full speed towards the enemy.

Whilst en route, a single masthead was sighted, believed at first to be an armed merchant cruiser perhaps acting as an outer screen for the convoy. *Scheer* closed rapidly and fired several warning shots from its secondary armament, ordering the vessel not to transmit, heave to and present papers. It was the 5,389 GRT SS *Mopan* sailing independently, and its captain complied despite protests from his wireless officer who pleaded to be allowed to warn inbound HX84. Successfully abandoned and the crew taken prisoner, *Mopan* was sunk by gunfire.

Krancke had lost valuable time in this diversion and did not sight HX84 until 1630hrs, *Scheer* approaching from dead ahead until only 17,000m distant whereupon *Scheer* turned broadside and opened fire with main guns at the sole escort, armed merchant cruiser HMS *Jervis Bay*. As secondary batteries fired at a tanker, the hopelessly outgunned *Jervis Bay* swung to port and returned fire, more to distract *Scheer* than any hope of inflicting damage. *Jervis Bay*'s Captain Edward Fegen ordered his convoy to scatter and the uneven battle lasted for 22 minutes, before *Jervis Bay* was battered beneath the waves, taking Fegen and most of his crew to the bottom.[10] Only 68 of the 254 crew were later picked up by a Swedish freighter, three of them subsequently dying from wounds.

The scattering convoy laid smoke and in the failing light *Scheer* was able to sink only five of its 37 merchant ships thanks to *Jervis Bay*'s gallant stand. By then *Scheer* had fired half of its secondary battery ammunition and a third of the main battery's ammunition. The Arado aircraft had also taken an estimated 40 per cent damage from small arms fire during the battle, and so Krancke ordered the action broken off and headed west to disguise his later intention to proceed towards the South Atlantic.

As desired by SKL, the attack on HX84 caused the recall of two further Halifax convoys and posting of battleships HMS *Nelson* and *Rodney* to block the Denmark Strait, while two battlecruisers, three light cruisers and six destroyers were despatched from Scapa Flow to patrol the Biscay approaches to Brest and Lorient. Three hunting groups were formed to hunt *Scheer*, occupying two carriers and five cruisers. North Atlantic convoys were henceforth to be accompanied by at least one battleship among its escort.

---

10 Fegen was subsequently awarded the Victoria Cross posthumously for his actions.

While *Admiral Scheer* had been in action, heavy cruiser *Admiral Hipper* was also readied for its inaugural Atlantic mission. Following action and the repair of damage sustained off Norway, *Hipper* had been earmarked for a major role in the aborted invasion of England under the fresh command of 48-year-old veteran *Kapitän zur See* Wilhelm Meisel. Its planned task was to divert the Home Fleet by supporting a feint attack on Scotland. However, following Operation *Sealion*'s cancellation, *Hipper* was instead ordered to the Atlantic to keep pressure on Allied convoys. An initial attempt in late September to break into the North Atlantic was thwarted by an engine room fire which left the ship powerless and drifting for four hours. Following nearly a full month of repairs in Hamburg, *Hipper* underwent training in the Baltic until 18 November before being readied for another attempt.

In his operation, code-named *Nordseetour* (North Sea Tour), Meisel was under orders to sail into the North Atlantic undetected and engage enemy convoy traffic before retreating to Brest, which had been designated the primary Kriegsmarine base in western France in October 1940. He was firmly instructed not to engage solo-sailing ships and to adhere to standing orders that forbade engaging enemy forces either superior or equal in strength.

Admiral Hipper sailed from Brunsbüttel on 30 November under torpedo boat escort. In worsening weather – perfect conditions for Meisel – *Hipper* passed through the Denmark Strait undetected on the night of 6 December, headed to rendezvous with tanker *Friedrich Breme* that lay on station off southern Greenland. Once refuelled, *Admiral Hipper* patrolled the presumed Halifax convoy route, consuming more fuel than expected in extremely harsh weather and suffering a temporary starboard engine failure. After a miserable and unsuccessful search, Meisel refuelled again from *Friedrich Breme* before laying course for Brest on 20 December. Four nights later, the unexpected traces of multiple ships were detected by the radar 700 miles west of Spain's Cape Finisterre. Concluding that this was likely to be a weakly escorted OB convoy that shuttled from Great Britain to West Africa, Meisel planned to attack the following morning.

At 0603hrs on Christmas Day, German lookouts spotted the convoy in poor weather conditions, with strong winds and rain squalls. Approaching unobserved, a heavy escorting cruiser was sighted first and Meisel opted to attack with a spread of torpedoes and disable the escort before attacking the convoy body. However, the attack failed and after opening fire with main guns, *Admiral Hipper* soon found itself in action against the heavy cruiser HMS *Berwick* supported by light cruisers HMS *Bonaventure* and *Dunedin* as part of the heavy defence for troop convoy WS5A comprising 11 troopers and eight munitions ships headed to Egypt. The convoy immediately began to scatter and as his secondary batteries scored hits on two merchants – *Empire Trooper* and SS *Arabistan* (killing two men) – Meisel obeyed standing orders to disengage, believing the approaching light cruisers to be destroyers and manoeuvring to avoid a suspected torpedo attack.

Thedor Krancke, photographed here after promotion to *Konteradmiral* in April 1941. He had captained *Admiral Scheer* on what would be the most successful surface raider Atlantic mission; successfully returning to Germany after having sunk Armed Merchant Cruiser HMS *Jervis Bay*, 14 merchant ships totalling 83,984 GRT and capturing two other tankers that reached France under command of their prize crews. (AC)

As *Admiral Hipper* successfully broke away, hits were scored on *Berwick* that disabled X-turret and a 4in gun of its secondary batteries, as well as holing the cruiser below the starboard waterline, causing some flooding. Four British sailors were killed and one severely wounded. Attempts by the Royal Navy's Gibraltar-based Force H to hunt for *Admiral Hipper* were fruitless and, despite running low on fuel and experiencing continued engine problems, Meisel stumbled upon 6,078 GRT British SS *Jumna* north of the Azores bound for Freetown. This commodore ship from dispersed convoy OB260 was immediately shelled and sank with all 64 crew and 44 passengers killed. On the evening of 27 December, *Admiral Hipper* entered Brest harbour; the first major Kriegsmarine surface ship to do so.

1941

Following the attack on HX84 *Admiral Scheer* had been replenished by *Nordmark* and headed towards the mid-Atlantic, beginning a spree of sinkings that would culminate in the Indian Ocean north-east of Madagascar on 22 February 1941 when Krancke sank his fourteenth ship, Dutch freighter SS *Rantaupandjang* carrying 4,000 tons of coal from Durban to Singapore. Four ships had been taken as prize, two used as temporary supply ships and then sunk, the remaining two tankers safely reaching France with prize crews aboard. Krancke, awarded the Knight's Cross on 21 February, had also successfully rendezvoused during the voyage with auxiliary cruisers *Thor* and *Atlantis*, and with U-boat U124. Suggestions by SKL that *Scheer* operate in conjunction with *Thor* were soundly rebuffed as *Scheer*'s presence would rob the disguised cruiser of its camouflage and sailing in tandem with *Thor* would rob the *Scheer* of its speed.

Admiral Scheer was shadowed by a Walrus aircraft launched by HMS *Glasgow* following the sinking of *Rantaupandjang* but managed to evade both it and the reinforced hunting group despatched by Vice Admiral Ralph Leatham, commander of the Royal Navy's East Indies Station. Krancke returned to the Atlantic and sailed without incident to the Denmark Strait, narrowly evading cruisers HMS *Fiji* and *Nigeria* before reaching the North Sea once more on 27 March and anchoring in Grimstadfjord two days later. An escort of two destroyers and a torpedo boat accompanied *Scheer* back to Germany, where Krancke dropped anchor at Kiel on 1 April 1941. After 161 days at sea, *Admiral Scheer* had sunk an armed merchant cruiser, 14 merchant ships totalling 83,984 GRT of shipping and captured two tankers that arrived in France carrying 15,970 tons of crude oil and 4,770 tons of fuel oil between them. Krancke departed command of *Admiral Scheer* in June 1941 and after a variety of staff postings became Chief of MGK West in April 1943.

As *Scheer* rampaged off south-west Africa, Admiral John Tovey, commander of the Royal Navy's Home Fleet, received disturbing intelligence on the evening of 25 January: two German battleships had been sighted passing through the Great Belt into the North Sea. Immediately, the main body of the Home Fleet, led by

Tovey's flagship HMS *Nelson*, departed Scapa Flow to take up position south of Iceland and prevent another German raider from breaking out into the Atlantic. Facing them were *Scharnhorst* and *Gneisenau* under the control of Fleet Commander *Admiral* Günther Lütjens and on the cusp of commencing Operation *Berlin*. This was their second attempt at launching the operation, the first thwarted in late December by storm damage suffered by Lütjens' flagship *Gneisenau*, captained by *Kapitän zur See* Otto Fein (previously Chief of Staff at MGK East), that had forced the mission aborted for repairs.

The *Admiral Scheer* photographed in the South Atlantic. (AC)

The objective of this new initiative had not altered from those of its predecessors. However, this time there would be two battleships operating in tandem, attacking the North Atlantic convoy route to overwhelm escort forces with superior firepower and then destroy merchant ships. Lütjens was, however, still constrained by the dogged mantra of 'no unnecessary risks' if faced with equal or superior forces. Nonetheless, Lütjens believed that Royal Navy battleships which B-Dienst had reported attached to convoy traffic, would only accompany them part of the way lest they lose cover provided by their own shorter-range anti-U-boat escort. To reinforce Operation *Berlin*, *Admiral Hipper* was to sail from Brest and attack the Gibraltar and West African convoy lanes, further confusing the enemy and dividing their defensive naval strength.

Seven supply ships had already been strategically positioned within the Arctic and North Atlantic and after a protracted game of cat and mouse

ADMIRAL SCHEER MEETS *ATLANTIS* AND *TANNENFELS*, EAST OF MADAGASCAR, 14 FEBRUARY 1941 (overleaf)

Admiral Scheer had proceeded from the South Atlantic into the Indian Ocean originally not only because it was deemed a potential theatre of operations, but also because it was a transit point to the Antarctic area. There *Kapitän zur See* Theodor Krancke hoped to intercept three valuable Norwegian whale factory ships and capture them. However, the activities of auxiliary cruisers and *Scheer* in the South Atlantic forewarned the US coastguard of this possibility and, despite their 'neutrality', they instructed the Norwegians to withdraw to South American ports. *Scheer* was ordered by SKL to remain in the Indian Ocean and meet with the auxiliary cruiser *Schiff 16 'Atlantis'* and refuel from the captured Norwegian tanker *Ketty Brøvig*. Though

they successfully met and officers from *Atlantis* managed to board *Scheer*, winds approaching hurricane strength forced the ships to relocate to calmer waters 300 miles further south before the refuelling could commence. Once they reached their new destination, *Scheer* replenished its fuel bunker while selected crew from *Atlantis* boarded the heavy cruiser.

Exchanging gifts, the entire crew of *Admiral Scheer* was given a fountain pen each from stock *Atlantis* had captured during its cruise, while *Scheer*'s crew presented 150,000 fresh eggs taken from the British refrigeration ship *Duquesa*, captured on 18 December.

with Tovey's searching ships in appalling weather, *Scharnhorst* and *Gneisenau* both passed undetected through the Denmark Strait on the night of 3 February, refuelling from the tanker *Schlettstadt* off Southern Greenland two days later. For the first time in history, German battleships were at large in the Atlantic. Meanwhile, having needed five weeks of repairs, *Admiral Hipper* left Brest as planned for its new thrust southwards in support of Operation *Berlin*.

At dawn on 8 February *Kapitänleutnant* Wolfgang Kähler, chief gunnery officer aboard *Gneisenau*, reported convoy HX106 700 miles east of Halifax and the two battleships separated; *Scharnhorst* to attack from the south, *Gneisenau* the north-west. However, Kähler's opposite number aboard *Scharnhorst*, *Kapitänleutnant* Wolf Löwisch, spotted the aged battleship HMS *Ramillies* escorting the convoy. Even though only *Ramillies* and a single corvette comprised the convoy defence, Lütjens felt compelled to break off the attack in view of his strict instructions to avoid enemy capital ships. Aboard *Scharnhorst*, *Kapitän zur See* Kurt-Caeser Hoffmann attempted to draw *Ramillies* away so that *Gneisenau* could attack, but failed and was later reprimanded by Lütjens for flouting Raeder's strict orders. Fortunately for Lütjens, only *Scharnhorst* had been sighted, and misidentified as either the *Hipper* or *Scheer*, Tovey sailing once more to block the heavy cruiser's expected return route to Germany or France while Force H from Gibraltar was diverted to cover the North Atlantic.

Aboard *Hipper*, Meisel had been allowed the freedom to attack independently sailing merchants and lightly defended convoys. Only three days from Brest, *Hipper* refuelled from the tanker *Spichern*, a captured Norwegian tanker converted to Kriegsmarine use. As the crew were inexperienced, Meisel let some of his engineers board the tanker to instruct the crew as they refuelled repeatedly over the following few days.

Closer to Gibraltar, five Focke-Wulf Fw. 200s had attacked convoy HG53 in cooperation with U37 which had encountered the convoy off Cape St Vincent. Clausen sank two ships before shadowing and transmitting position reports for both the Luftwaffe and *Hipper*. Condors bombed and sank four ships, heavily damaging a fifth, while one Fw. 200 hit by anti-aircraft fire crash landed in Portugal. U37 sank freighter *Brandenburg* on 10 February and, though attempts to bring *Hipper* into action against the main body of HG53 failed, Meisel found straggling freighter SS *Iceland* the following day and sank it with shellfire. For the first time a capital ship, U-boat and aircraft had cooperated in action with degrees of success.

That evening, *Hipper*'s radar picked up traces of unescorted convoy SLS64 of 19 ships, Meisel shadowing overnight before beginning his attack at 0615hrs from the western dark side of the horizon. Lookouts aboard the lead freighter in the port column, SS *Margot*, were first to report an unidentified 'mano'war' before *Hipper* opened fire and began to cleave through the merchant ships. Aboard SS *Warlaby*, Convoy Commodore Captain Septimus Murray hoisted the 'T4' signal for the convoy to disperse as SS *Shrewsbury*, heading Column 2, was already taking direct hits.

Over the next hour Meisel sank a confirmed seven freighters and severely damaged three others, though he recorded 13 ships sunk, apparently signalling one intact vessel to stop and pick up survivors as he departed. During the attack, *Hipper* had fired all torpedoes, over two-thirds of its main gun high-explosive ordnance and a considerable amount of its secondary battery ammunition. Defensive fire from merchantmen had registered no damage, though Meisel, low on ammunition and fuel and fearing that British forces would block his planned voyage to the Azores region to replenish, opted to return to Brest. This raised some eyebrows in Berlin as SKL tartly replied: 'Assume pressing reasons for return. Otherwise fuel and re-ammunition from *Breme* and remain at sea.'

Regardless, on 14 February *Hipper* entered Brest harbour once again, entering the smaller dry dock and damaging its starboard screw on uncharted wreckage while doing so, causing delays in becoming seaworthy once more as a spare had to be shipped from Kiel. Meisel received the Knight's Cross later that month as the Royal Air Force began a series of air raids aimed at the cruiser. Although inflicting no serious damage, the attacks convinced Raeder to bring *Hipper* back to Germany quickly, avoiding the time of the expected appearance of *Admiral Scheer* at the Denmark Strait. Meisel sailed from Brest on 15 March and reached Kiel after 13 days, making the voyage completely undetected. The ship would never return to the Atlantic.

Confirming February as the most successful month for the German raiders, Lütjens positioned *Scharnhorst* and *Gneisenau* astride the western edge of the Halifax convoy route and the two battleships found themselves repeatedly encountering independently sailing merchant ships. Unable to avoid detection, Lütjens instead allowed attacks; *Gneisenau* sinking four and *Scharnhorst* one, both accumulating a growing number of prisoners. Radio jamming had silenced all but one of the merchants attacked and, correctly surmising that the Royal Navy was now aware of the battleships' presence further west than expected, Lütjens ordered both ships to the south-east, refuelling as they went.

ADMIRAL HIPPER ATTACKS CONVOY SLS64, 12 FEBRUARY 1941 (overleaf)

Kapitän zur See Theodor Meisel had been attempting to find convoy HG53, which had already been successfully attacked by Luftwaffe Fw200 'Condor' aircraft in cooperation with *Kapitänleutnant* Nicolai Clausen's U37. Despite sinking a straggling freighter, Meisel failed to locate the body of the convoy but that same evening *Admiral Hipper*'s radar detected ships, at first thought to be the target convoy, but soon discovered to be unescorted SLS64 bound for Liverpool. Shadowing the convoy during the hours of darkness, Meisel attacked as dawn was breaking, approaching from a dark horizon. The attack lasted an hour in which seven merchant ships were sunk – SS *Warlaby*, the Commodore's ship, was sunk second with all but four of the 39 people aboard surviving. In total, the attack killed 147 people.

Jim Laurier

At this time *Vizeadmiral* Karl Dönitz had reinvigorated his South Atlantic operations and earmarked three large Type IXB U-boats to operate off West Africa. At 1410hrs on 7 March Dönitz received notice that northbound convoy SL67 had been sighted by *Scharnhorst* and *Gneisenau*, which were shadowing without attacking due to the presence of battleship HMS *Malaya* in the escort alongside destroyers HMS *Faulknor* and *Forester*, armed merchant cruiser HMS *Cilicia* and corvette HMS *Asphodel*.

Georg-Wilhelm Schulz's U124 contacted *Scharnhorst* and *Gneisenau* and plans were laid for both U124 and U105 to attack SL67 with the intention of sinking or at least damaging *Malaya*, clearing a path for the two German battleships. With U106 a few days behind the other boats, the latter was to position itself to pick up remnants of the convoy. During the early morning on 8 March both U-boats attacked, sinking five merchant ships but failing to hit *Malaya*. Later that day the British sighted the two German battleships which were briefly chased, but outpaced pursuit and withdrew west away from the convoy which was soon reinforced with Force H as escort.

By this point both battleships were experiencing mechanical problems, *Gneisenau*'s most serious as the boiler superheaters were defective and damaged. Headed north once more, Lütjens met with tankers *Ermland* and *Uckermark* which were kept in loose company to enlarge the available scouting radius. It was in this configuration that they discovered a bounty of merchant ships sailing from dispersed westbound convoys. *Scharnhorst* sank six ships, while *Gneisenau* sank seven and captured three tankers as prizes: two plundered and then sunk and the third, MT *Polykarp*, reaching the Gironde River on 24 March with a prize crew aboard. Though they did not realise it, these were the final Atlantic successes of the Kriegsmarine's major surface ships.

Lütjens had been ordered to cease operations by 17 March in deference to *Hipper* and *Scheer*'s return through the Denmark Strait and he at first opted to sail for the Canary Islands as a diversionary measure. However, fresh instructions to head for Brest were received in order that the two battleships may be prepared for a future operation with new battleship *Bismarck* and cruiser *Prinz Eugen* scheduled for April. Despite a brief sighting by British reconnaissance aircraft and reinforcement of Royal Navy forces before Biscay, the two battleships successfully entered Brest harbour under escort by three *Sperrbrecher*

The 'sisters'; *Scharnhorst* (left) and *Gneisenau*. Germany's most successful battleships that operated in the North Sea until breaking into the Atlantic in February 1941 during Operation Berlin. (AC)

and two torpedo boats. *Gneisenau* rounded Pointe de Petit Minou at 0700hrs before moving gingerly into Basin Number 8 at Laninon and later that afternoon its sister-ship steamed into the Rade de Brest, Lütjens soon returning to Berlin to take command of impending operations by *Bismarck*.

Air Raids

The British Admiralty discovered the whereabouts of *Scharnhorst* and *Gneisenau* on 27 March with the aid of a coded message from newly recruited French Resistance member Jean Philippon, code-named 'Hilaron'. Philippon had been the Second Officer on French submarine *Ouessant*, scuttled in the Penfeld before the Germans' arrival in June 1940. Continuing to work under armistice arrangements within the confines of the Arsenal, he had access to the exact locations of the German ships and, by extension, so did the RAF.

The RAF had first begun bombing the French ports in September 1940, but the presence of the major ships caused a marked escalation. British bombers began a long series of heavy air raids against the battleships and while the dry-dock basin for *Gneisenau* was being drained an unexploded bomb from one such raid was found between the stocks. The decision was made to move *Gneisenau* from its perilous position until the arrival of Luftwaffe bomb disposal specialists from Morlaix, temporarily mooring the battleship in the inner military harbour. Unfortunately, *Gneisenau* was moored without the benefit of extensive torpedo net protection which could not be provided at that time, nor with the addition of a *Sperrbrecher* or other steamer of sufficient draught secured alongside to seaward for additional protection. The decision had been taken not to do so as the available buoy to which *Gneisenau* would be tethered could not withstand the stress of such a load and nearby anchoring could not be carried out due to the seabed conditions and strong tidal ebb and flow combined with near storm-force winds, forecast to intensify. However, two *Sperrbrecher* were secured to the inside of the harbour mole after security consultation with *Seekommandant Bretagne*, who also ordered significant reinforcement by the motorized light 2cm flak weapons of 5. *Marine Flak Abteilung* 803 along the harbour mole.

On 6 April, RAF Coastal Command No. 22 Squadron, based at St Eval in Cornwall, ordered six aircraft to attack the exposed *Gneisenau*; three with torpedoes and three carrying mines designed for the destruction of anti-torpedo netting. However, pouring rain reduced the grass airstrip to a quagmire of mud. Two of the mine carriers failed to take off, the last getting lost in heavy rain over the sea. Of the torpedo aircraft, one also became lost in miserable weather conditions and the two remaining aircraft were separated due to thick mist over the sea, one eventually turning back for Cornwall. Only Beaufort number OA-X/22 flown by Flying Officer Kenneth Campbell reached the planned rendezvous point west of Brest.

Campbell was only 23 years old, born and raised in Saltcoats, Scotland, and had already successfully torpedoed the merchant ship SS *Widar* in the

Wadden Sea near Borkum less than a month before. Described as fearless and aggressive in attack, this mission marked his twentieth operational sortie and he was accompanied by 19-year-old Canadian observer from Toronto, Sergeant Jimmy Scott, RCAF; wireless operator 31-year-old Sergeant William Mulliss and 22-year-old Londoner Flight Sergeant Ralph Hillman as air gunner.

As Campbell circled the rendezvous point there was no trace of any other Beauforts and with dawn beginning to lighten the eastern sky he decided to make his attack run through the narrow Goulet de Brest strait and onwards to the target.

The sky was gradually lightening over the harbour despite heavy cloud cover and mist; visibility 1,000m at best in what German lookouts noted as very hazy conditions despite a brisk north-north-east breeze, freshening as the sun rose. Aboard *Gneisenau* a full complement of flak gunners were at their post and the ship's watch officer was on the bridge as Campbell's aircraft suddenly appeared over the harbour mole at 0710hrs, only 600m distant from the battleship.

Campbell had approached from the south at low altitude between the cliffs of the Crozon Peninsular and the northern fringe of the Goulet de Brest and passed over the mole with only 15–20m to spare before any defending shots were fired. An officer aboard *Gneisenau*, walking past the starboard 10.5cm flak guns, later recalled seeing the torpedo drop; the first defensive firing beginning as the torpedo hit the water at a range of only 100m. Despite *Gneisenau*'s starboard 3.7cm flak weapons managing 67 shots, and 2cm guns another 297 shots, the Beaufort banked hard to starboard aiming to recross the mole and retrace its course before combined intense fire from three of the 24cm guns situated on the mole hit the port engine which immediately caught fire. The aircraft lunged briefly upward before crashing nose first into the inner harbour, fuel tanks exploding and the fuselage broken in two to sink to the seabed. There were no survivors and, while

Halifax bombers from 35 Squadron, RAF, bombing the major ships at Brest on 18 December 1941, as part of Operation *Veracity*. In total 18 Halifaxes, 18 Stirlings and 11 Manchester bombers took part in the daylight raid, with seven bombers lost (five to defending Bf 109 fighters, two to flak). *Prinz Eugen* is visible at the far right, moored to the harbour wall with protective torpedo nets to seaward, with *Scharnhorst* and *Gneisenau* both in dry docks at the left, both draped in camouflage netting. Smoke screens are beginning to obscure the port, special naval smoke units have been moved to Brest. (CBW/Alamy Stock Photo)

the bodies of Hillman and Mulliss were found floating in the water, four days later the wreckage was recovered with the remaining two men still strapped into their seats. They were buried by the Germans with full military honours.

However, the German gunners' victory had come too late for the targeted battleship. The torpedo struck the *Gneisenau*'s starboard side level with compartment IV and caused serious damage to the reserve command centre as well as flooding generator and turbine housings. After the attack and as the stormy conditions ebbed, a *Sperrbrecher* was taken alongside *Gneisenau* lest a repeat attack be made, and security reinforced by minesweepers and patrolling *U-Jäger*. Yet, the appearance of a photo-reconnaissance Spitfire high above the port was the only further aircraft sighted that day.

Returned to dry dock on 10 April, the ships were targeted by further heavy Allied air raids launched against the port. As a result of one such raid on 11 April by a combined force of Blenheim, Wellington and Manchester aircraft from eight different squadrons, *Gneisenau* suffered four direct hits from bombers (one of the bombs a dud) causing substantial damage and killing 78 men with another 84 wounded, 10 of whom later died of their injuries. Amidst the destruction wrought, all accommodation decks forward of compartment XII were rendered uninhabitable by blast damage and fire, and aside from normal harbour watches and flak gunners, the crew were moved ashore to quarters in Douarnanez.

Meanwhile, in Germany, the newest 'pride of the fleet', *Bismarck*, was now fully operational and Raeder carefully deliberated whether it should be sent to sea at the earliest possible moment or await the full commissioning of sister ship *Tirpitz* to allow a combined Atlantic action by Germany's two most powerful battleships. There were several issues to be considered. The United States remained neutral and British air power could not yet cover the full

BEAUFORT OA-X/22 LAUNCHING A TORPEDO AGAINST *GNEISENAU*, BREST HARBOUR, 6 APRIL 1941 (overleaf)

Flying Officer Kenneth Campbell and his three-man crew launched an audacious solo attack on *Gneisenau* just as dawn broke over Brest harbour on 6 April 1941. The ship had been reported by a French agent as having been moved from its dry dock at 0900hrs the previous day and moored, unprotected, in Brest's military harbour. The use of an anti-torpedo net would be considered almost mandatory in such circumstances, but Brest's naval arsenal could not provide one specifically for *Gneisenau* as stocks had been used up on spanning the entrance channel to the main harbour basin. The warship's location was confirmed by photo-reconnaissance Spitfire and the attack launched. It was planned to comprise six Beaufort bombers but reduced to one by weather conditions. All four of the Beaufort's crew were killed when their bomber was shot down, but not before the torpedo struck *Gneisenau* on the starboard stern causing extensive damage. Over 3,000 tons of seawater flooded the hull causing a two-degree list to starboard as well as damage to the propulsion system. The concussion of the explosion significantly disrupted the ship's electrical system.

Jim Laurier

Flying Officer Kenneth Campbell, killed along with his crew after torpedoing *Gneisenau* on 6 April 1941. The loss of the crew was not confirmed until 20 May by the International Red Cross. Flying Officer Campbell was awarded the Victoria Cross posthumously for his action on 13 March 1942. King George VI presented the medal to Campbell's parents at Buckingham Palace on 23 June 1943, the first VC awarded to a pilot of Coastal Command. The remainder of the crew remained, unfairly, unrecognized. (Pump Park Vintage Photography/Alamy Stock Photo)

Atlantic as the U-boat war raged in both northern and southern areas. In the Mediterranean the *Afrika Korps* was going into action in North Africa and the invasion of Greece was imminent, so diversion of Mediterranean Royal Navy strength elsewhere could seriously alter events.

Buoyed by the successes of *Scheer* and *Hipper*, Raeder's confidence was high and he decided on immediate deployment in company with the new cruiser *Prinz Eugen*. As part of the plan, both *Scharnhorst* and *Gneisenau* were also to put to sea and commence parallel operations from Brest, though the persistent engine trouble aboard *Scharnhorst* and bomb and torpedo damage inflicted on *Gneisenau* negated their ability to sail as planned.

However, in conference on 25 April with Lütjens, the latter urged delay until at least *Scharnhorst* was fit to sail once more. Lütjens enjoyed Raeder's complete confidence as a master tactician and experienced commander, though he was perhaps something of a conflicted man. Lütjens was one-quarter Jewish and understandably was not fond of National Socialism or his new Führer. Also, like Raeder, he had privately despaired at the outbreak of war with Britain fearing that Germany's lack of resources, particularly oil, would render defeat inevitable.

In discussion with Raeder, Lütjens was unrestrained in his opinion that *Bismarck*'s operation should be postponed, not least of all because *Prinz Eugen* had struck a British aerial magnetic mine two days previously which had damaged the fuel tank, propeller shaft couplings and fire control equipment, and would require three weeks of dockyard time to repair. However, as weeks passed, nights were getting gradually shorter for any potential passage through the Denmark Strait. The Wehrmacht was also gearing towards war with the Soviet Union; a struggle that would undoubtedly consume the fuel and resources needed for large-scale naval operations. Mindful of the strategic picture, Raeder remained adamant that the time to place additional pressure on the Royal Navy was now. Though Lütjens may have harboured grave misgivings about the venture – named Operation *Rheinübung* – he departed the conference having reached a professional accord with his commander and began making final plans for *Bismarck*'s voyage.

The story of what followed is well told elsewhere but the bare facts are that *Prinz Eugen*, commanded by *Kapitän zur See* Helmuth Brinkmann, had left Gotenhafen on 18 May with *Bismarck*. Detected by various threads of Allied intelligence from the outset, Operation *Rheinübung* made a promising start just after control of the two ships was transferred from Naval Group North to Naval Group West. On 24 May there occurred the storied Battle of the Denmark Strait and destruction of HMS *Hood*. However, the damaged *Bismarck* was harried and hunted by strong Royal Navy forces and Lütjens detached *Prinz Eugen* under cover of a rain squall to head south and begin its raiding mission.

British intelligence believed Brest to be the eventual destination for *Bismarck*, not least of all after 'Hilaron' had reported the construction of two huge concrete mooring blocks in 30m of water near the Aulne Estuary. These could only mean the arrival of a ship displacing 35,000 tons or over, the blocks later nicknamed by the French the *Ducs de l'Aulne*. However, *Bismarck* was repeatedly engaged by carrier aircraft and enemy ships, becoming progressively more damaged and eventually unable to steer. Finally, completely incapacitated, *Bismarck* scuttled off the coast of France on 27 May with the loss of Lütjens, its captain Ernst Lindemann and all but 114 out of a crew of over 2,200 men.

As this played out, *Prinz Eugen* urgently required fuel and MGK West coordinated a meeting with *Spichern* before the cruiser headed south. The ship was, however, experiencing myriad mechanical problems, compounded by *Spichern*'s supplied fuel being contaminated with a high saltwater content and 5 per cent other contaminants resulting in boiler failures and heavy, shock-like bursts of dense smoke. Following a second refuelling from *Esso Hamburg*, Brinkmann opted to remain located between the two tankers until the '*Bismarck*

A photograph taken from the deck of an escorting vessel that shows *Gneisenau* and *Scharnhorst* heading in line through the English Channel during Operation *Cerberus*. *Prinz Eugen* is presumably out of shot to port of this vessel. (Naval Heritage and History Command)

alarm' simmered down, using the two tankers as extended scout ships. An American coastguard cruiser was reported nearby by MGK West and Brinkmann opted to move further south, hunting for independent merchant ships, but he was to be foiled by recurrent mechanical difficulties that included a malfunctioning port engine turbine, problems with cooling of the middle engine and a damaged starboard screw that reduced speed. His War Diary noted the only conclusion available on 29 May: 'Unlike auxiliary cruisers I have no disguise. I have only one weapon, which is my higher speed. Not only has this attribute become questionable, but I have already been robbed of 20% and I can no longer fulfil my assigned mission. I have made the decision to head for harbour for repairs. A return via Iceland is absolutely impossible … nothing is left but to head for

The forward turrets of *Prinz Eugen*. The turret tops had been painted red during its time in the Baltic, repainted blue for Operation *Cerberus*. (Maidun Collection/Alamy Stock Photo)

With Brest under heavy bombardment, the cruiser and battleship crews not needed aboard were billeted inland, primarily around Douarnenez. The Kriegsmarine placed great importance on crew welfare ashore and, in general, their relations with the local population were cordial at that stage of the war. (United Archives GmbH/Alamy Stock Photo)

a French harbour in Biscay.' On 1 June *Prinz Eugen* entered Brest harbour.

The presence of three large warships in Brest provoked a renewed surge in the bombing of the harbour city and *Prinz Eugen* was next to be hit, killing 50 men and immobilizing the ship. Only *Scharnhorst* was able to leave Brest during July, for exercises near La Rochelle. However, it was not to remain unscathed and returned to Brest suffering a 7-degree list to starboard after being hit in a bombing attack, codenamed Operation *Sunrise*, by nine RAF No. 35 Squadron Halifax bombers. Two of these nine were shot down as well as half of the accompanying six Halifaxes belonging to No. 76 Squadron, which failed to achieve any hits upon their own targets. Constant damage meant that the ships would not be capable of Atlantic operations again until the year's end at the earliest. Raeder also pointed out in conference with Hitler that the ships' crews would require exercises and training to bring them to full readiness, taking several weeks and only possible in Biscay, near Brest.

However, Hitler had become increasingly – and vocally – disillusioned with capital ship warfare since the loss of *Bismarck*. He was fixated on war in the East and his own strong beliefs that British and American troops were planning to invade Norway, turning his Northern flank and upsetting the flow of raw materials from Scandinavia to Germany. Even recommendations from Raeder in November 1941 that *Admiral Scheer*, fit for operations once more, be sent to the Atlantic were refused on the grounds that the cruiser would best be used to protect Norway. Finally, in conference on 29 December, Hitler declared that the Brest ships would be best used to protect Norway and if this proved impossible, they should be decommissioned and their guns and crews used to reinforce ground forces there.

DEFENSIVE STRUCTURES APPROACHING BREST

Brest had long been an established French military port and German occupiers frequently took advantage of existing fortifications and captured weapons to bolster coastal defence. As well as torpedo netting strung across the narrow Goulet de Brest and four searchlight emplacements at the waterline along the Goulet, the following naval coastal artillery (*Marine Artillerie Abteilung*) and naval flak batteries (*Marine Flak Abteilung*) were emplaced by 1942. The original Luftwaffe flak batteries that had covered the harbour in the early stages of the occupation had been largely replaced by Kriegsmarine units. During 1943 and 1944, extra Kriegsmarine coastal artillery and flak units were positioned around the city, augmented by Army batteries that were in place as the US Army attacked the city in September 1944.

Legend:

Marine Flak Abteilung

Marine Artillerie Abteilung

○ Stp Re 311-FuMB 'Donau' radar site
1./3. FuMAbt – Funk Mess Abteilung

Battery 'Holzendorf'
1./MAA 262

'Graf Spee' Battery
5./MAA 262

Toulbroch Battery

Batterie du Minou

Batterie du Mengant

Batterie du Dellac

Barge 356
4x torpedo tubes

Portzig 2./
3./MaFIA 803

Portzig 5./
MaFIA 803

6./MaFIA 803

Brest Arsenal 'Dingi'
3./MaFIA 803

Brest Naval School

Batterie du Kerbonn
4./MAA 262

Batterie du Toulinguet

Kermeur
1./MaFIA 805

Pointe du Grand Couin
H.K.B 1274 K.V.
Gruppe Camaret

Pointe du Cornouaille
1./MaFIA 804

Batterie des Capucins

Batterie du Fort Robert

Batterie Pointe des Espagnoles

Rade de Brest

Tremet battery

6./MaFIA 804

Île Longue
3./MaFIA 804

5./MaFIA 804

Kertanguy
2./MaFIA 804

'Bismarck Blocks'

Keroual 'Zwischendeck'
2./MaFIA 803

Kerognant 'Vormars'
4./MaFIA 803

Rochglas
4./MaFIA 805

Forestic
3./ MaFIA 805

Mermerien
2./MaFIA 805

Kerziou
4./MaFIA 804

Kermeur
1./MaFIA 805

BREST

Guipavas Luftwaffe base

Lanveoc seaplane base

Lanveoc: The Lanveoc base was an old French seaplane base occupied by III/KG40 (part of *Fliegerführer Atlantik*) under Major Walther Herbold, which used Heinkel He 111 aircraft. *Obit. Josef Saumweber*, Helmut Lorenz and Friedrich Müller of 1./KG.126 pioneered the use of torpedoes there from He 111 aircraft. From 1943, Bf 110 aircraft from ZG1 occupied the field.

The Kriegsmarine constructed two huge concrete mooring blocks in 30m of water near the Aulne Estuary. They were used by *Gneisenau* and the *Prinz Eugen* at various times for mooring during gunnery tests. Named by the French the '*Ducs de l'Aulne*' (Dukes of the Aulne), today as the 'Bismarck Blocks', we know them as the 'Bismarck Blocks'.

1942

Prinz Eugen's bow during Operation *Cerberus* showing two of the extra *Vierling* 2cm quad anti-aircraft guns fitted to the ship for the break though the Channel. (AC)

The position of the large German ships at Brest was indeed becoming untenable; Bomber Command mounted no fewer than 11 operations of varying sizes against the port during January alone. By then Hitler's decision was absolute. In his words, the situation of the warships was that of 'a patient with cancer who is doomed unless he submits to an operation'. Even the ships' 'flypaper' attraction to bombers that were otherwise diverted from attacking Germany would only last until they were incapacitated. The culmination of Hitler's inflexible will was an almost suicidal plan to send the three German ships dashing up the English Channel to Germany with strong Luftwaffe and Kriegsmarine escorts, right under the noses of the British – and in broad daylight.

The planned transit of the large ships would take 14 hours to complete and would be made with no preparatory training to alert British intelligence. The British Admiralty had indeed anticipated such a move and on 29 January photographic reconnaissance revealed the arrival at Brest of extra destroyers, torpedo boats and minesweepers. By 8 February photographs revealed *Scharnhorst* and *Prinz Eugen* in harbour and warnings were issued to RAF units regarding pending departures. Nevertheless, they expected any such break out attempt to be made under cover of darkness and the British were completely caught off-balance. They had failed to detect the complicated minesweeping patterns that had been undertaken by various flotillas stretching along the French Channel coast and missed the departure of the ships from Brest when *Scharnhorst*, *Gneisenau* and *Prinz Eugen*, under destroyer and torpedo boat escort, cleared the Brest net barrage at 2245hrs on 11 February. Their exit had been delayed by a British bombing raid on Brest, unwittingly providing further camouflage, as did faulty equipment aboard patrolling radar-equipped RAF aircraft.

With overall control by Saalwächter and MGK West, *Vizeadmiral* Otto Ciliax (C-in-C of German battleships) had immediate command of the

THE THREE CAPITAL SHIPS AND ESCORTING FORCES OF OPERATION *CERBERUS*

Organized and controlled by *Generaladmiral* Alfred Saalwächter at MGK West headquarters in Paris, *Cerberus* began at 2245hrs on 11 February 1942. It was a complicated operation that pulled in nine minesweeping flotillas, four *Vorpostenboot* flotillas and *Sperrbrecher 145* of *Vizeadmiral* Friedrich Ruge's security forces, as well as one destroyer flotilla, three torpedo boat flotillas and three S-boat flotillas. Overhead, Luftflotte 3 provided three fighter squadrons and a single night fighter squadron – Bf 109s, Fw 190s and Bf 110s – in rotating shifts for continuous cover. The main procession, led by Z29 of 5. Destroyer Flotilla, comprised *Scharnhorst*, *Gneisenau* and *Prinz Eugen* steaming at full speed in line. Overlapping *Vorpostenboot* flotillas created outlying picket lines as the procession passed, unable to match their speed.

Prinz Eugen

Gneisenau

Scharnhorst

Torpedo boat screen

Torpedo boat screen

Destroyer screen

S-boat screen

Vorpostenboot
picket ships

Constant air
patrols

Leading destroyer Z29

Pre-swept channel
cleared by
minesweeping
flotillas and
Sprerrbrecher

Destroyer Z29 leads the *Cerberus* procession through the Channel. Aboard Z29 was *Kapitän zur See* Erich Bey, C-in-C of Destroyers (*Führer der Zerstörer*). *Flottenche*f Otto Ciliax transferred to Z29 after *Scharnhorst* struck a mine. (World History Archive/ Alamy Stock photo)

operation that was code-named *Cerberus*. The Luftwaffe's Luftflotte 3 provided thick fighter protection (Operation *Donnerkeil*) with a continuous strength of 16 fighters to be maintained by relay over the ships during the hours of daylight and a larger reserve force on immediate standby. This support was controlled by *Oberst* Adolf Galland, with Luftwaffe liaison officer, *Oberst* Max Ibel, aboard the *Scharnhorst* to direct operations. One destroyer flotilla, three torpedo boat flotillas and three S-boat flotillas accompanied the ships, supported by 11 security flotillas that ran the length of the English Channel.

Not until 1042hrs did patrolling Spitfires sight the *Cerberus* procession and the air and naval attacks that followed were hindered by poor coordination, bad weather and fierce German defence that inflicted significant casualties. While the Luftwaffe lost 22 aircraft, the Kriegsmarine lost only the small 292-ton *Vorpostenboot V1302 John Mahn* which was hit and sunk by two bombs from a Coastal Command Hudson with 12 crewmen killed. A hint of disaster loomed when both *Scharnhorst* and *Gneisenau* struck mines previously laid by Bomber Command; the first disabling *Scharnhorst* for 30 nerve-wracking minutes just beyond Dover. In low cloud cover, the ship was not located before engine power returned, though Ciliax had already transferred to Z29 to resume the voyage. By midday on 13 February, the three ships were docked in Germany. Though *Cerberus* was a success and a humiliating blow to British prestige, the Kriegsmarine major surface Atlantic presence was no more.

ANALYSIS

What had begun as an attempt to create an ocean-going battle fleet capable of combat with the French and Royal Navies had morphed into a means by which to wage war on Britain's maritime commerce. This lack of clarity of purpose did the Kriegsmarine a huge disservice but was not solely limited to that branch of service. The entire German war machine was riven with internal problems, the roots of which could fairly claim to be in Hitler's divisive style of leadership. The three main services were in perpetual competition for increasingly scarce resources and manpower for both the construction of weapons and machinery and the ability to effectively man them. With the Waffen SS added to this contest, and leaders of the Luftwaffe and army more politically adept than the archly conservative Raeder, the Kriegsmarine frequently came off the worst of all the services.

Hitler was famously fascinated by capital ships as examples of naval power and national prestige and could recite technical specifications and details of naval vessels and armament. However, he never fully appreciated the navy's role or its potential in the war against the West, Britain in particular. His military vision was of continental land war with particular emphasis on spreading to the East. He had a genuine admiration for Britain's colonization of 'lesser races' in nearly every corner of the globe but failed to grasp how essential it was to maintain a strong naval power to both take, and hold, this empire. With his limited strategic vision, everything was viewed through the prism of supporting an army on the march. Indeed, the Luftwaffe was formed around its ability to tactically support ground forces, with no eye to a more global strategy. Just as Hitler misunderstood the possibilities presented by dominating the Mediterranean Sea through successful occupation of North Africa and subsequent exploiting drives through the Middle East, he failed to allow the Kriegsmarine major surface units to realize their full potential as surface raiders.

Though arguably not always utilizing the best designs for such a role, the Kriegsmarine was still capable of inflicting grievous damage and extreme confusion and concern on its opposing number. But once its naval commanders were hamstrung in their ability to act, lest German prestige be damaged by the loss of another capital ship, their viability as offensive commerce raiders was effectively curtailed. The difficulties that could have been imposed on the Royal Navy by pursuit of skilfully operated and daring raiders within the Atlantic and Indian Oceans is not to be underestimated. The brief flashes of such operations that were successfully undertaken by such ships as *Admiral Graf Spee* and *Admiral Scheer* show what might have been had they been given greater freedom of operation, not so much by MGK West, but by the supreme commander who gradually assumed more and more that mantle of supreme warlord as every year passed. Even the exhaustive hunt for the *Bismarck* proved what strength could be diverted from other theatres of action to find a single German capital ship.

In total, the surface raiders (excluding auxiliary cruisers) destroyed 286,580 GRT of enemy merchant shipping in the Atlantic and Indian Oceans and captured three tankers that were sailed intact to occupied France with their precious cargoes. Though an impressive figure, compare the fact that U-boats sank 113 merchants totalling 732,884 GRT (as well as ten enemy warships) during their most successful single month of November 1942. Was it a wasted effort by the surface fleet? No, although it is also worth noting that the construction of *Scharnhorst* cost 143.5 million Reichsmarks. For that price, three Type VIIC U-boats could be constructed. In a country of finite resources, it is hard to reconcile the expenditure in money, materials and manpower to construct a surface fleet the use of which during most of the war was predominantly that of a *potential* threat, rather than an actual one.

It is true that Germany entered the war woefully unprepared as Hitler failed to succeed in 'just one more

The *Bismarck* prepares for its maiden voyage. Undoubted pride of the German Fleet and an impressive ship, *Bismarck* was not wholly suited to its role as commerce raider. (Shawshots/Alamy Stock Photo)

political gamble' when he invaded Poland. All three services of the Wehrmacht were underequipped to deal with a war of the scale that it quickly became, particularly the Kriegsmarine. U-boat strength was less than 20 per cent the number that Karl Dönitz claimed he needed to fight a successful war on Britain's merchant shipping. Light forces such as destroyers and torpedo boats were woefully lacking in both number and ocean-going ability and major ships were few; the vestiges of an idea to create a 'balanced fleet' that would be ready for any potential war nearly a decade later than when it came. The repurposing of existing ships, and those soon to be completed, from naval threat to commerce raider was difficult and not always successful. Likewise, the rethinking of orthodox naval strategic thought took root in some naval officers more than others. However, even those men who rose to the task of captaining successful Atlantic raiders were suddenly under severe operational restraints as their supreme commander fretted about the potential damage to Germany's morale by the loss of any ship in action. Hitler viewed *Graf Spee*'s destruction as a disaster caused by a lack of fighting spirit as Langsdorff refused to slug it out with the enemy and go down gloriously fighting with the sacrifice of his young crew. He failed to see the rationale for the ship's scuttling, nor remember the tonnage accrued by *Graf Spee* in action nor the extreme dislocation that Langsdorff had caused to British and French naval forces as well as merchant convoys. The 1941 destruction of the *Bismarck* provided the final nail in the coffin of independently minded raiding operations that could risk all for higher potential reward.

Instead, those Atlantic ships still available were withdrawn to fend off imaginary threats to Norway. It is true that their position was precarious – the Luftwaffe also having begun the war understrength and without clear purpose and, having been degraded by years in action, was unable to ward off enemy bombing raids on such targets as Brest. However, the retreat to Germany in late 1942 of the last major surface forces, though rightly celebrated as an audacious tactical victory, was in fact a major strategic defeat. No longer was there an Atlantic threat other than that posed by U-boats, which were themselves already fighting a losing battle. With the Atlantic cleared of major German surface ships, the Allied navies operating within that theatre were free to concentrate their full attention on countering the U-boats. For their part, though there would be brief moments of triumph for Dönitz's men, the U-boats would not reach the kind of strength that they had required to effectively blockade Great Britain until they had already lost the war at sea; bested by evolving Allied tactics, code-breaking and technological advances. Meanwhile, those surface forces left for MGK West by the end of 1942 were either coastal security units, or, in the case of destroyers and torpedo boats, were so few that they became little more than defensive escort ships.

Scharnhorst during Operation *Cerberus*. The smoke at left is from the battleship's main guns which were fired against surface threats during the break through the Channel. *Prinz Eugen* had even used its main guns in 'Bruno' and 'Caesar' turrets as anti-aircraft, firing at British torpedo bombers. (Ullstein Bild/Getty Images)

FURTHER READING

Barnett, Correlli, *Engage the Enemy More Closely*, Hodder & Stoughton, London, 1992.

Bekker, Cajus, *Swastika at Sea*, William Kimber, London, 1953.

Bird, Keith W., 'The Origins and Role of German Naval History in the Interwar Period' *1918–1939*, *Naval War College Review*, vol. 32, no. 2, Rhode Island, March–April 1979.

Bohn, Roland, *Raids Aeriens Sur la Bretagne Durant La Seconde Guerre Mondiale, 1 & 2*, Thematic Studies and Research in Finistère and Brittany, Brest, 2000.

Bohn, Roland and Le Berre, Alain, *Chronique D'Hier, Tome II*, Self-Published, Brest, 1994.

Bowyer, Chaz, *Men of Coastal Command 1939–1945*, William Kimber, London, 1985.

Buffetaut, Yves, *Les Ports de l'Atlantique 1939–1945*, Marines Éditions, Rennes, 2003.

Chazette, Alain and Reberac, Fabian, *Kriegsmarine*, Éditions Heimdel, Bayeux, 1997.

Churchill, Winston, *The Second World War*, 6 vols, Cassell & Co. London, 1954.

Griffiths, Denis, *Steam at Sea*, Conway Maritime Press, London, 1997.

Haarr, Geirr, *The Gathering Storm: The Naval War in Northern Europe*, Seaforth Publishing, London, 2012.

Jacquin, Frederic, *Les Bombardements de Brest 1940–1944*, Éditions MEB, Saint-Thonan, 1997.

Kahn, David, *Hitler's Spies*, Da Capo Press, Boston, 1978.

Kennedy, Ludovic, *Pursuit*, Collins Sons & Co., London, 1974.

Lohmann W. and Hildebrand H. H., *Die Deutsche Kriegsmarine 1939–1945*, 3 vols, Podzun Verlag, Bad Nauheim, 1956.

Mallmann Showell, Jak P., *Fuehrer Conferences on Naval Affairs*, Chatham Publishing, London, 2005.

Martienssen, Anthony, *Hitler and his Admirals*, Secker and Warburg, London, 1959.

Paterson, Lawrence, *Hitler's Forgotten Flotillas*, Seaforth Publishing, London, 2017.

Paterson, Lawrence, *The U-Boat War*, Osprey Publishing, London, 2022.

Raeder, Erich, *Grand Admiral*, De Capo, 2001. First published as *My Life*, USNI, 1960.

Rohwer, J. and Hümmelchen, G., *Chronik des Seekrieges 1939–1945*, Gerhar Stalling Verlag, 1968.

Sellwood, A. V., *Atlantis*, Werner Laurie, London, 1955.

Whitley, M. J., *Cruisers of World War Two*, Arms and Armour Press, London, 1995.

INDEX